EVIDENCE
FOR
JESUS

Timeless Answers for
Tough Questions about Christ

JOSH MCDOWELL & SEAN MCDOWELL

Thomas Nelson
Since 1798

THOMAS NELSON

Evidence for Jesus
Copyright © 2023 by Josh McDowell Ministry

Published in Nashville, Tennessee, by Thomas Nelson. Thomas Nelson is a registered trademark of HarperCollins Christian Publishing, Inc.

Thomas Nelson titles may be purchased in bulk for educational, business, fundraising, or sales promotional use. For information, please email SpecialMarkets@ThomasNelson.com.

ISBN 978-0-310-12424-5 (softcover)
ISBN 978-0-310-12426-9 (audio)
ISBN 978-0-310-12425-2 (ebook)

Cover design: LUCAS Art & Design
Interior design: Sara Colley

Printed in the United States of America

23 24 25 26 27 28 29 30 31 32 /TRM/ 14 13 12 11 10 9 8 7 6 5 4 3 2 1

CONTENTS

SECTION 3: WHY JESUS IS UNIQUE

SECTION 4: JESUS IS NOT A COPYCAT SAVIOR

SECTION 5: HOW JESUS FULFILLS OLD TESTAMENT PROPHECY

SECTION 6: EVIDENCE FOR THE RESURRECTION OF JESUS

SECTION 7: WHY THE RESURRECTION OF JESUS MATTERS

ACKNOWLEDGMENTS

THE IMPORTANCE OF KNOWING THAT CHRIST IS WHO HE claimed and to be able to effectively communicate that truth makes us all the more grateful for the numerous people who have spoken into this project.

First and foremost, deep appreciation to Timothy Fox, who worked closely with me (Sean) to take the complexities of the more in-depth *Evidence That Demands a Verdict* and transform them into this easily accessible work.

Thanks to Daniel Marrs, who originally foresaw the potential of such a work and planted the seed of possibility. We are grateful to Stan Gundry, Ryan Pazdur, and others at HarperCollins who understood the appeal of this concept, took Daniel's vision, and put it into motion.

Many thanks to Dale Williams, acquisitions editor at HarperCollins, for skillfully guiding this book through the editing process to completion. Dale's valuable insights and wisdom were crucial in the shaping of this work. And our thanks to Kim Tanner for being a remarkably skilled and attentive editor.

Finally, thanks to Dr. Titus Kennedy and Dr. Jonathan McLatchie for offering critical feedback on the manuscript. You both improved this book tremendously.

INTRODUCTION

WELCOME TO *EVIDENCE FOR JESUS*. WHETHER YOU ARE A Christian or a skeptic, we're thrilled you are joining us for this journey into the historical evidence for the life, death, and resurrection of the most influential person who has ever lived: Jesus of Nazareth.

While this book is a father-son project, we thought it would be helpful to begin with my (Josh's) story. Sean's story will come at the end. As a teenager, I was haunted by three big questions: Who am I? Why am I here? Where am I going? I desperately wanted answers to these questions, so as a young student, I started searching for meaning in popularity, business success, sports, school, and other avenues. But everything I tried left me empty and without answers.

Everything changed when some Christian friends challenged me, a prelaw student, to make a rigorous intellectual examination of the Christian faith. They challenged me to consider a few questions: Did God truly enter the human race in the person of Jesus, who died for the sins of humanity? Can we trust the Bible as true? Did Jesus really rise from the dead? And can Jesus really change a life today?

I accepted their challenge—just to prove them wrong. I decided to write a book that would show them that Christianity was a joke, intellectually and historically. Since this was long before the internet and at a time when there were hardly any apologetics books on the historical Jesus, I left college for a period of months so that I could travel throughout the United States and Europe to gather evidence in libraries and museums to prove that Christianity was a sham. But through my studies, I realized there was no escaping the facts: the Bible is reliable, there is historical evidence for the resurrection of Christ, and Jesus really did claim to be God. I then decided to put Christ's claims to the supreme test. I became a Christian.

This decision changed my life. Through studying Scripture and the loving mentorship of a pastor, I developed the capacity to love people and sought to serve them instead of use them. I had a terrible temper, but that began to fade. I was able to forgive my father, a raging alcoholic who had torn my family apart. God even gave me the strength to offer forgiveness to the man who sexually abused me as a child. Here's the bottom line: the kind of evidence for Jesus that we explore in this book got my attention. But it was coming to understand the love of God, and his kindness, that drew me to become a believer (See Romans 2:4).

Why do I tell you all this? Because what each of us concludes about the identity of Jesus is the most important decision we will ever make. Let me say this again to make sure it sinks in: *What we conclude about the identity of Jesus is the most important decision we will ever make.* This is why Jesus asked, "Who do you say that I am?" (Mark 8:29). Our answer to this question has implications for how we live our lives and for our eternal destinies. We hope this book will have the kind of impact on you that our examination of the evidence has had on us.

Here's a quick overview of the evidence we will explore in this book. Section 1 explores the sources we use to examine the historical Jesus, considering both biblical and extrabiblical sources. Section 2 seeks to discover who exactly Jesus of Nazareth was, looking at the claims he made about himself, as well as the claims his closest followers made about him. Section 3 considers the uniqueness of Jesus in comparison with other religious figures.

Section 4 examines a popular objection from the online community of skeptics, that Jesus is just a copycat of other dying and rising gods from the ancient Near East. Section 5 addresses the evidence that Jesus fulfilled prophecy, responds to some common objections, and discusses why prophecy matters.

Sections 6 and 7 examine the most important event of human history: the resurrection of Jesus. We will look at key historical facts such as the death, burial, and appearance stories of Jesus and consider whether any naturalistic hypotheses can account for these facts as well as for the resurrection. In section 7, we explore why the resurrection matters for both Christian theology and the practice of the Christian life.

This book can be used for individual study, group study, or in a classroom. It is not written primarily for scholars, but rather for both believers and skeptics who want to begin a journey into the historical evidence for Jesus. If you want further study, we recommend you check out our more in-depth book, *Evidence That Demands a Verdict*.

Finally, we hope you will read, study, and share what you discover in this book with family, friends, neighbors, and those online. Are you ready? Let's begin!

THE HISTORICAL EVIDENCE FOR JESUS

WHEN I (JOSH) RESEARCHED FOR THE FIRST EDITION OF *Evidence That Demands a Verdict* in 1972, I did not include a chapter on the existence of Jesus. Why not? As far as I could tell, there was little doubt Jesus existed. I certainly had no problem concluding Jesus was real. The primary question was not *if* Jesus existed but whether he claimed to be God and rose from the dead.

The vast majority of scholars today—across a wide range of perspectives and disciplines—collectively believe Jesus was *at least* a historical figure who lived and died in the first century AD. Even the agnostic New Testament scholar Bart Ehrman has written a book defending the existence of Jesus: *Did Jesus Exist? The Historical Argument for Jesus of Nazareth.*

Yet on a popular level, largely because of the ubiquity of the internet and social media, many people have come to question Jesus's existence. So let's look at the evidence that Jesus was real.

CHAPTER 1

CAN WE USE THE BIBLE FOR HISTORICAL EVIDENCE OF JESUS?

ONE OF THE MOST COMMON CHALLENGES TO THE RELIABIL-ity of the New Testament is that the documents are unreliable because they are biased. In one sense, this is a fair charge. Yet not all biases are equal. The apostles had biases. John admits that he wrote his gospel in part so that readers will believe in Jesus (John 20:31). Some biases can cause people to distort the truth, but others can motivate them to proclaim truth. In the case of John, who was an eyewitness of the life, death, and resurrection of Jesus, we believe it motivated him to carefully preserve the truth (John 21:24–25).

When it comes to the historical Jesus, the vast majority of sources we have for the historical Jesus are Christian. Naturally, people may reject such sources because they assume Christian documents are biased. But doesn't this show an unfair bias against Christian sources? Accusations of bias can cut both ways. Consider the example of Holocaust survivors. Such individuals would undoubtedly be biased. But this does not in itself provide good reason to discount their testimony. We must be open-minded to the possibility that Christian sources are historically reliable testimonies to the historicity of Jesus and consider them as part of a larger, cumulative case. As with Holocaust survivors, we should not reject Christian testimonies outright. In this chapter, we will consider what the New Testament documents reveal about the existence of Jesus. Later we will consider further claims about his identity and miracles.

NEW TESTAMENT DOCUMENTS

The Gospels

The authors of the four gospels don't argue for Jesus's existence—they assume it. They want the reader to know that their accounts are reliable (e.g., John 21:24), but their focus is to convince readers that Jesus, whom they knew, is God and should be followed.

Many skeptical scholars question whether every story about Jesus contained in the Gospels actually took place. Yet those who don't believe in the authenticity of every story in the Gospels still affirm that Jesus existed. Agnostic New Testament scholar Bart Ehrman is skeptical about the supernatural accounts surrounding Jesus's life. But this does not lead him to deny the existence of Jesus. After examining the Gospels, as well as the traditions from which they arose, Ehrman concluded, "The vast network of these traditions, numerically significant, widely dispersed, and largely independent of one another, makes it almost certain that whatever one wants to say about Jesus, at the very least one must say that he existed."[1]

The gospel accounts provide sufficient New Testament evidence to conclude that Jesus existed. But there's more. Let's move on to the writings of Paul.

Paul

The apostle Paul, once a persecutor of Christians, changed dramatically into a missionary who tried to bring more people to the faith. His letters don't contain a complete picture of Jesus's life because they are occasional letters designed to address specific concerns within the churches to which he wrote. Still, Paul clearly based many arguments on the assumption that Jesus did exist. His writings are important because they are likely the earliest Christian documents and the earliest writings we have concerning Jesus as a historical person. Even critical scholars accept that Paul wrote seven of the letters attributed to him (Galatians, 1 Corinthians, 2 Corinthians, Romans, Philemon, Philippians, and 1 Thessalonians). Let's examine five things that Paul affirms regarding Jesus's life:

FACT	REFERENCE	COMMENT
Paul believed Jesus was born	Gal. 4:4; Rom. 1:3	Jesus was born of a woman, descended from David
Paul believed Jesus spoke	1 Cor. 7:10–12	Paul cites Jesus's teaching on divorce and expounds on it
Paul believed Jesus died	Direct claims or allusions in nearly all his writings	Jesus's death (a public crucifixion for anyone to see) was central to Paul's teaching

FACT	REFERENCE	COMMENT
Paul believed Jesus rose from the dead	Specific references in nine of his thirteen letters	In 1 Cor. 15, Paul mentions that many people (including himself) saw the risen Jesus, and encourages doubters to ask them
Paul believed there were contemporary witnesses to Jesus	Gal. 1:18–20; 1 Cor. 9:5; 1 Cor. 15:6–8	Paul mentions meeting James the brother of Christ, Peter, and others who met Jesus

On top of the five things listed in the previous chart, in their book defending the historicity of Jesus of Nazareth, *The Jesus Legend*, theologians Paul Rhodes Eddy and Gregory A. Boyd offer a list of historical facts that Paul affirms about Jesus's life and ministry. Paul knew that Jesus

- was born and raised as a Jew (Gal. 4:4)
- was a descendant of Abraham and David (Rom. 1:3; Gal. 3:16)
- had a brother named James (Gal. 1:19)
- possibly had other brothers as well (1 Cor. 9:5)
- had numerous disciples (1 Cor. 9:5)
- was betrayed (1 Cor. 11:23) and executed by crucifixion (1 Cor. 1:17–18; Gal. 5:11; 6:12; Phil. 2:8; 3:18) with the help of some Judean Jews (1 Thess. 2:14–15)

- instituted the Lord's Supper the night before his death (1 Cor. 11:23–25)
- was buried and resurrected three days later (Rom. 4:24–25; 1 Cor. 15:4–8; 2 Cor. 4:14; Gal. 1:1; 1 Thess. 4:14)
- was meek, gentle, self-sacrificial, and humble (2 Cor. 10:1; Phil. 2:5–7)
- lived a model life that should be imitated by all (1 Cor. 11:1)[2]

In addition to this list, Paul also recognized that Jesus taught on marriage and divorce (1 Cor. 7:10) and that he testified before Pontius Pilate (1 Tim. 6:13). In sum, Paul and the people to whom he witnessed believed in a literal, historical Jesus who lived, ministered, died, and rose again on the third day.

EARLY CHRISTIAN CREEDS

Early Christian creeds also provide evidence for the historical Jesus. Now, by creeds we don't mean the cherished belief statements often recited in churches such as the Apostles' Creed or the Nicene Creed. We mean the teachings and sayings that the earliest Christians shared among themselves before the New Testament was even written. Several of the early creeds were incorporated into the New Testament by Paul and other New Testament authors. These creeds are some of the first glimpses we have into early Christian beliefs. Let's explore some.

Philippians 2:6-11

Philippians 2:6–11 is a "pre-Pauline hymn" that references Jesus's divine and human nature. Jesus took on the "nature of a servant" (NIV) and "human likeness" (NIV), humbling himself "as a man" to die on the cross. Here, Jesus's human nature is clearly contrasted with his divine nature, thus providing evidence that Jesus walked the earth as a flesh-and-blood human being.

2 Timothy 2:8 and Romans 1:3-4

Second Timothy 2:8 sets forth two aspects of Jesus's life. Here Jesus's birth in the lineage of David is presented along with his resurrection from the dead, showing the early Christians' interest in linking Jesus to history. Similarly, Romans 1:3–4, plausibly an ancient, pre-Pauline creed, juxtaposes the man Jesus "born of the seed of David according to the flesh" to the divine Jesus whose claims were vindicated by his rising from the dead. For our purposes, we need note only the early interest in Jesus's earthly, physical connections, as he was born of a descendant of David's family.

1 Timothy 3:16

Like the others, the ancient creed in 1 Timothy 3:16 begins by affirming that Jesus became a human, showing how Jesus's humanity was an important aspect of Christianity from the beginning. From this and other relevant texts, we can glean several important facts about the events in Jesus's life: Jesus was born as a human (Phil. 2:7; 1 Tim. 3:16; 1 John 4:2) of the line of David (Rom. 1:3; 2 Tim. 2:8), and his teachings were spread throughout the world, leading others to believe in him (1 Tim. 3:16).

1 Corinthians 15:3–7

1 Corinthians 15:3–7 contains what may be the most important New Testament creed for the study of the historical existence of Jesus. Although this passage specifically addresses Jesus's resurrection, it also provides information for a broader examination of the historicity of Jesus, mentioning his death, burial, and alleged appearances to many people.

The key to this passage's importance is its early date, with 1 Corinthians believed to have been written around 54 or 55 AD. Even the most critical scholars across the entire theological spectrum recognize this as an early Christian creed that predated Paul. If Jesus died around 30 AD, this letter, by a major church leader who knew people who accompanied Jesus during his earthly ministry, was written within twenty-five years of Jesus's death. And if this letter contains earlier tradition that Paul received and is passing on, then belief in the death, burial, and appearances of Jesus exists fewer than twenty-five years from the death and resurrection of Jesus.

One reason for the widespread support of the idea that Paul is relaying an ancient creed is Paul's use of the words *delivered* and *received* in setting up his report. Paul states that he is passing on content that he received from another, meaning a tradition that was passed down to him. Paul believes tradition is important and carries authority, which he makes clear in numerous passages. Recall that Paul was once a Pharisee, a group that had a great zeal for tradition, as reported by Mark and Josephus.

In addition, right after this creed, verse 11 seems to indicate that the Corinthians understand Paul's proclamation of the core tenets of the gospel—the death, burial, and resurrection of Jesus—and that it reflects the testimony of the other apostles. Since the Corinthians were acquainted with the preaching of Peter (See 1 Cor. 1:12), there is good reason to believe that the core claims about Jesus trace back to the original disciples of Jesus.

In sum, we can be confident that 1 Corinthians 15:3–7 contains early tradition that minimally confirms the existence of Jesus. Combined with verse 11, we can conclude that belief in the existence of Jesus (and his death, burial, and resurrection) traces back very early in the church.

CONCLUSION

It's clear that the biblical authors were not writing about a fictional person, but about a real, flesh-and-blood human they saw, interacted with, and followed. They aren't the only early Christians who provide evidence about the historical Jesus, however. Let's explore some early writings from outside the Bible.

CHAPTER 2

IS THERE EVIDENCE FOR JESUS OUTSIDE THE BIBLE?

WHEN WE HAVE CONVERSATIONS WITH PEOPLE ABOUT THE historical Jesus, many ask for non-Christian sources. This is a fair request because if Jesus lived and did the things the Bible records about him, we would expect some additional sources. Yet, as we indicate in chapter 4, we would both believe the gospel accounts of Jesus even if there were no extrabiblical sources. And the reason is simple: *the New Testament documents can be trusted.* But with that said, let's consider extrabiblical sources for Jesus, which provide corroborative evidence for the gospel accounts and minimally help establish that Jesus existed. In particular, let's look at the two most important ancient non-Christian sources for evidence of the historical Jesus: Cornelius Tacitus and Flavius Josephus.

TACITUS

Cornelius Tacitus was a Roman historian who lived approximately AD 56 to 120. Many scholars consider him the greatest Roman historian and see the *Annals* as our best source of information for the time surrounding the life of Jesus. His

Annals covers the time of the Roman emperors Augustus through Nero. Though not all of *Annals* survives, one passage that does is key to our study.

In AD 64 there was a devastating fire for which many people believed Nero was responsible. To stop the public outcry, Nero blamed the Christians. Tacitus explains what happened:

> Consequently, to get rid of the report, Nero fastened the guilt and inflicted the most exquisite tortures on a class hated for their abominations, called Christians by the populace. Christus, from whom the name had its origin, suffered the extreme penalty during the reign of Tiberius at the hands of one of our procurators, Pontius Pilatus, and a most mischievous superstition, thus checked for the moment, again broke out not only in Judaea, the first source of the evil, but even in Rome, where all things hideous and shameful from every part of the world find their centre and become popular.[1]

This passage confirms various points from the Gospels, such as the existence of Jesus and Pontius Pilate, Jesus's crucifixion ("the extreme penalty"), and possibly the belief in Jesus's resurrection ("a most mischievous superstition"). It also provides a general date of the crucifixion ("during the reign of Tiberius") as well as locations of the early spread of Christianity (Judea and Rome). Thus, this passage of Tacitus is vital for understanding the origin of Christianity. But there are potential objections to the authenticity and trustworthiness of this text.

Forgery?

Could Tacitus's text be a forgery? Or, at the very least, could Christians have snuck in information locating Jesus as a historical person? This is highly unlikely for three reasons:

1. Tacitus clearly despises Christians. If a Christian altered the document, he probably wouldn't have been so offensive toward Christians.
2. The passage doesn't specifically mention the resurrection, something a Christian editor would have been eager to include.
3. The style of the text is seamless, meaning there doesn't seem to be any evidence of someone editing the text.

Use of the Term *Procurator*

One might argue against the reliability of Tacitus's account since he refers to Pilate as "procurator," which is the term used in Tacitus's day, instead of "prefect," the title that would have been used in Pilate's time. However, Tacitus may have used the term *procurator* simply for the sake of his audience. There's also evidence that the terms *procurator* and *prefect* were used fluidly in the first century. Both Philo and Josephus refer to Pilate as "procurator," just like Tacitus, and Josephus uses the terms *procurator* and *prefect* interchangeably in his writings.[2]

"Christ" Instead of "Jesus"

Does Tacitus's reference to "Christ" ("Christus") instead of "Jesus" show that he relied on Christian testimony instead of independent witnesses? If so, this could discredit him as a source of independent information about Jesus. But remember that Tacitus *despised* Christians. It's unlikely that a man considered so reliable would then rely on a group he hated for information. By the early second century, "Christ" and "Jesus" were used interchangeably by Christians and non-Christians alike. Thus, we ought not assume that Tacitus relied solely on Christians for his information.

We can be confident that this passage from Tacitus's *Annals* is authentic. It provides additional historical reporting that affirms important events recorded in the New Testament and adds significant value toward confirming the existence of the historical Jesus from sources outside Scripture. While we don't know the source Tacitus relied on for his information about Jesus, we do know he considered it reliable enough to include in his writings. Thus, it should be part of our larger case for the existence of Jesus. Now let's look at our second important non-Christian source of information.

JOSEPHUS

Flavius Josephus was a Jewish politician, soldier, and historian who lived around AD 37–100. He's considered the most important Jewish historian of ancient times. Josephus wrote *Antiquities of the Jews* to explain the Jewish people and their beliefs to Romans to reduce anti-Jewish bigotry. Two passages in *Antiquities* are important in our investigation of the historicity of Jesus.

Antiquities 20.200
In *Antiquities* 20.200, Josephus writes about the death of Jesus's brother James at the instigation of the high priest Ananus,

a bold man in his temper, and very insolent; he was also of the sect of the Sadducees, who are very rigid in judging offenders, above all the rest of the Jews, as we have already observed; when, therefore, Ananus was of this disposition, he thought he had now a proper opportunity [to exercise his authority]. Festus was now dead, and Albinus was but upon the road; so he assembled the Sanhedrin of judges, and brought before them the brother of Jesus, who was called Christ, whose name was James, and some others.... He delivered them to be stoned.[3]

Undoubtedly, this is one of the most significant non-Christian passages relating to the historical Jesus. Josephus verifies that a man named James was put to death, that he was Jesus's brother, and this Jesus was called the Christ. The reference to Jesus and James is simple and matter of fact, which lends to its credibility. But, of course, the passage has its detractors, and so its authenticity must be defended against criticism.

Paul Rhodes Eddy and Gregory A. Boyd's book *The Jesus Legend* offers a thoughtful response to the hypothesis that the Jesus of Christianity is merely a legend, while providing substantive evidence that Jesus is a true historical figure. Although they view the case against the James passage as "formidable," they conclude that the passage's authenticity is solid. The following are a few points Eddy and Boyd make regarding the previous Josephus passage:

1. Critics argue that there is little manuscript evidence for *Antiquities*. While that is true, it is comparable to that of other ancient works.

2. Josephus mentions "Christos" only in connection with Jesus, even though he writes about other messianic figures. Josephus mentions twenty-one other[4] people named Jesus, which makes it likely Josephus simply mentions that James's brother "was called Christ" to identify which James was killed.

3. Jesus is mentioned before James in the passage, which leads some critics to question why Josephus would choose to structure the passage in this way. Yet the structure does not elevate Jesus in such a drastic way as to make him the focus of the passage, and it appears to be a simple construction Josephus used for clarity.

4. Critics argue that the flow of the passage would not be interrupted if the information about Jesus was removed. While this may be true, it is hardly proof of a later Christian insertion.[5]

Accordingly, we should trust that this passage is authentic. Josephus offers a clear non-Christian attestation of the historicity of Jesus and agrees with the New Testament assertion that James was Jesus's brother.

Antiquities 18.63

Antiquities 18.63 is a passage commonly referred to as the *Testimonium Flavianum* and is much more open to debate concerning its authenticity than 20.200. Most scholars believe the passage is generally authentic but was modified by a Christian editor; thus, some scholars have attempted to discern what is authentic in this passage and what has been altered. For example, Bible scholar John P. Meier offers what he believes is the original Josephus passage:

> At this time there appeared Jesus, a wise man. For he was a doer of startling deeds, a teacher of people who receive the truth with pleasure. And he gained a following both among many Jews and among many of Greek origin. And when Pilate, because of an accusation made by the leading men among us, condemned him to the cross, those who had loved him previously did not cease to do so. And up until this very day the tribe of Christians (named after him) has not died out.[6]

Although Meier omits outright claims to Jesus being the Messiah, the text still includes important details about Jesus's life, such as Jesus being a wise teacher who did great deeds (miracles) and Pilate ordering his crucifixion.

Regardless of which words a scholar chooses to classify as late insertions, the bulk of the passage is seen by many scholars as authentic to Josephus. While we don't want to overstate the significance of this passage, when we combine it with *Antiquities* 20.200, there is good reason to conclude that it offers additional support for the historicity of Jesus.

CONCLUSION

There are other non-Christian sources of information about Jesus of Nazareth, such as Suetonius, Celsus, and Thallus, but Tacitus and Josephus alone suffice to establish Jesus's historicity. Have you wondered why there aren't more sources?

Wouldn't *everyone* in antiquity be talking about the alleged miracle worker who claimed to be God? Not necessarily. We're spoiled nowadays with easy access to information, thanks to the internet. If a significant event occurs, news instantly travels across the world. When it comes to ancient history, we don't have that luxury. But by standards accepted by scholars and historians, we have sufficient evidence to conclude that Jesus of Nazareth is a real person who walked the earth.

CHAPTER 3

ARE THERE CHRISTIAN SOURCES FOR JESUS OUTSIDE THE BIBLE?

SINCE THE FIRST SECTION OF THIS BOOK IS FOCUSED PRImarily on the existence of Jesus, it is fair to use all the available evidence, which includes biblical accounts, non-Christian accounts, and early extrabiblical Christian sources. There is a collection of writings from first- and second-century Christian leaders known collectively as the Apostolic Fathers. Their writings not only provide significant information about the early church, but several of them can be traced back to the apostles, providing helpful information for this study. Let's examine three of them.

CLEMENT OF ROME

First Clement is a letter written to the church at Corinth in the late first or early second century from the church at Rome. It is widely believed Clement knew the apostles, including Peter and Paul, and may even be the man mentioned in Philippians 4:3. First Clement includes a reference to Jesus and the early church:

The Apostles received the Gospel for us from the Lord Jesus Christ; Jesus Christ was sent forth from God. So then Christ is from God, and the Apostles are from Christ. Both therefore came of the will of God in the appointed order. Having therefore received a charge, and having been fully assured through the resurrection of our Lord Jesus Christ and confirmed in the word of God with full assurance of the Holy Ghost, they went forth with the glad tidings that the kingdom of God should come. So preaching everywhere in country and town, they appointed their firstfruits, when they had proved them by the Spirit, to be bishops and deacons unto them that should believe.[1]

In this passage is a description of movement from the delivery of the gospel to the apostles, to Jesus's resurrection, to the beginning of the fulfillment of the Great Commission wherein the apostles began missionary activity.

IGNATIUS

Ignatius was the bishop of Antioch and was condemned to death in Rome in the early second century. There are several historical references to Jesus in letters written by Ignatius, including *To the Trallians*:

Jesus Christ, who was of the race of David, who was the Son of Mary, who was truly born and ate and drank, was truly persecuted under Pontius Pilate, was truly crucified and died in the sight of those in heaven and those on earth and those under the earth; who moreover was truly raised from the dead, His Father having raised Him, who in the like fashion will so raise us also who believe on Him.[2]

Notice that Ignatius lays out several significant Christian doctrines, including that Jesus truly lived ("was truly born and ate and drank"), died, and rose from the dead.

In his epistle *To the Smyrneans*, he writes,

He is truly of the race of David according to the flesh, but Son of God by the Divine will and power, truly born of a virgin and baptized by John. . . .

For I know and believe that He was in the flesh even after the resurrection. . . . And straightway they [the apostles] touched Him, and they believed, being joined unto His flesh and His blood. . . . And after His resurrection He [both] ate with them and drank with them.[3]

In his letter *To the Magnesians*, Ignatius attempts to sway his readers' opinion:

Be ye fully persuaded concerning the birth and the passion and the resurrection, which took place in the time of the governorship of Pontius Pilate; for these things were truly and certainly done by Jesus Christ our hope.[4]

Ehrman sees Ignatius as a significant witness for the historicity of Jesus:

Ignatius, then, provides us yet with another independent witness to the life of Jesus. Again, it should not be objected that he is writing too late to be of any value in our quest. He cannot be shown to have been relying on the Gospels. And he was bishop in Antioch, the city where both Peter and Paul spent considerable time in the preceding generation, as Paul himself tells us in Galatians. His views too can trace a lineage straight back to apostolic times.[5]

POLYCARP

Polycarp was a student of the apostle John and knew of other apostles, which we learn from *his* student, Irenaeus:

> But Polycarp also was not only instructed by apostles, and conversed with many who had seen Christ, but was also, by apostles in Asia, appointed bishop of the Church in Smyrna, whom I also saw in my early youth, for he tarried [on earth] a very long time, and, when a very old man, gloriously and most nobly suffering martyrdom, departed this life, having always taught the things which he had learned from the apostles, and which the Church has handed down, and which alone are true.[6]

In his letter to the church at Philippi, Polycarp affirms many facts and doctrines about Jesus—namely, that he died and rose again (1:2), offered commandments (2:2), taught the Sermon on the Mount (2:3), will judge all (6:2), and was sinless (8:1).[7]

PAPIAS

Papias was a church father from the early second century. While none of his works have survived, they are mentioned in the writings of other Christian authors, such as the great Christian historian Eusebius. In *Church History* 3.39, Eusebius states,

> But Papias himself in the preface to his discourses by no means declares that he was himself a hearer and eyewitness of the holy apostles, but he shows by the words which he uses that he received the doctrines of the faith from those who were their friends.[8]

Papias interviewed anyone he met who knew the disciples, explicitly naming many of them. We see the names of two early church fathers in the following passage:

> If, then, any one came, who had been a follower of the elders, I questioned him in regard to the words of the elders—what Andrew or what Peter said, or what was said by Philip, or by Thomas, or by James, or by John, or by Matthew, or by any other of the disciples of the Lord, and what things Aristion and the presbyter John, the disciples of the Lord, say. For I did not think that what was to be gotten from the books would profit me as much as what came from the living and abiding voice. . . .
>
> And Papias, of whom we are now speaking, confesses that he received the words of the apostles from those that followed them, but says that he was himself a hearer of

Aristion and the presbyter John. At least he mentions them frequently by name, and gives their traditions in his writings.[9]

Papias also provides information that some believe confirms that Matthew and Mark are the true authors of the gospels containing their names:

> This also the presbyter said: "Mark, having become the interpreter of Peter, wrote down accurately, though not in order, whatsoever he remembered of the things said or done by Christ. For he neither heard the Lord nor followed him, but afterward, as I said, he followed Peter, who adapted his teaching to the needs of his hearers, but with no intention of giving a connected account of the Lord's discourses, so that Mark committed no error while he thus wrote some things as he remembered them. For he was careful of one thing, not to omit any of the things which he had heard, and not to state any of them falsely." These things are related by Papias concerning Mark.
>
> But concerning Matthew he writes as follows: "So then Matthew wrote the oracles in the Hebrew language, and every one interpreted them as he was able." And the same writer uses testimonies from the first Epistle of John and from that of Peter likewise. And he relates another story of a woman, who was accused of many sins before the Lord, which is contained in the Gospel according to the Hebrews. These things we have thought it necessary to observe in addition to what has been already stated.[10]

Although Papias may never have met Jesus or his disciples, he made sure to interview anyone he met who did know the disciples to glean whatever he could about the teachings of Jesus.

CONCLUSION

Clement and Ignatius are most important to our study, not only assuming a historical Jesus but going to great lengths to affirm key facts about his life on earth. Polycarp and Papias also provide important information about Jesus and what they learned from Jesus's disciples. Note that these writers are from the first and second centuries, and some of them may have known the apostles personally. So while these sources are not direct witnesses to the life of Jesus, they are very early, independent, and trustworthy.

CHAPTER 4

IS THE NEW TESTAMENT RELIABLE?

WHEN I (JOSH) WAS A SKEPTIC, SOME CHRISTIANS CHAL-lenged me to consider the claims of Christ. I honestly thought it was a joke and that such a task would be easy. To disprove Christianity, I knew I needed to find evidence against the reliability of the Bible. Surprisingly, after traveling to Europe and the Middle East to see some of the evidence with my own eyes, I began to reconsider my agnostic position. Eventually I concluded that the Bible—and in particular the New Testament—could be trusted as a historical source about Jesus. While the evidence goes far beyond what we can cover in this chapter, and much more evidence has come to light since my initial search, please allow us to introduce you to some of the evidence that the New Testament is reliable. Note that we're not asking whether the Bible is God's Word, whether it's inerrant, or anything like that. We simply want to know if we can trust the New Testament as a reliable account of history. Keep one last thing in mind: This chapter moves beyond the fact that Jesus existed to considering whether we can trust the

New Testament regarding the teachings, life, death, and resurrection of Jesus.

How will we approach this task? By the same criteria that other historical documents are tested. We will consider three tests: the bibliographical test, the internal evidence test, and the external evidence test. Let's begin by examining the New Testament to see how well it does with each test to determine its reliability as an accurate historical source.

Because the original copies of the New Testament books (known as autographs) have not been found, most of this chapter will examine the historicity of the early manuscript copies that were made from them, concentrating on the bibliographic test.

DATING THE FOUR GOSPELS AND ACTS

A full treatment on the dating of the four gospels and Acts are beyond the scope of this book. But it can be reasonably argued that all four biographies of Jesus in the New Testament, as well as the book of Acts, were written within a few decades—and certainly within a century—of the events they describe. Most scholars acknowledge this and place the canonical gospels and Acts securely within the first century. Nevertheless, even if late dating were correct, we would still have records of the events surrounding the origin of Christianity that are earlier than those sometimes used to support unquestioned events in history.

BOOK	EARLY DATE	LATE DATE
Matthew	50–75	75–120
Mark	45–65	65–80
Luke	60–80	80–110
John	65–90	90–140
Acts	62–80	80–130

THE BIBLIOGRAPHICAL TEST

The bibliographical test aims to determine the reliability of the transmission of an ancient writing. In other words, how reliable are the copies we have today? One way of approaching this is to look at the number of copies we have and the closeness of those copies to the original.

The Number of Manuscripts and Their Closeness to the Original

How many manuscripts of the New Testament do we have today? It's a large number that grows even larger as new discoveries are made. Accordingly, researchers and historians are constantly revising their estimates. Without question, the New Testament boasts the best attested manuscript transmission when compared with other ancient documents. The bibliographical test helps confirm that the New Testament has been accurately transmitted through the centuries. Here's a table of the number of New Testament manuscripts broken down by language:

NUMBER OF BIBLICAL MANUSCRIPTS

Language*	Earliest MS (old)	Earliest MS (new)	Number of MSS (old)	Number of MSS (new)
Armenian	AD 887	AD 862	2,000+	2,000+
Coptic	Late 3rd c. AD	Late 3rd c. AD	Around 975	Around 975
Gothic	5th or 6th c. AD	5th or 6th c. AD	6	6
Ethiopian	10th c. AD	6th c. AD	600+	600+
Total Latin translations Old Latin Vulgate	N/A 4th c. AD 4th c. AD	N/A 4th c. AD 4th c. AD	50 10,000+	110 10,000+
Syriac	5th c. AD	Late 4th or Early 5th c. AD	350+	350+
Georgian	Late 9th c. AD	5th c. AD	43+	89
Slavic	10th c. AD	10th c. AD	4,000+	4,000+
Total non-Greek manuscripts				18,130+
Greek	AD 130 (or earlier)	AD 130 (or earlier)	5,838	5,856
TOTAL GREEK AND NON-GREEK MANUSCRIPTS				23,986

Biblical Manuscripts, Scrolls, and Translations	
New Testament Greek manuscripts	5,856
New Testament early translations	18,130
Old Testament scrolls, codices	42,300**
TOTAL BIBLICAL MANUSCRIPT EVIDENCES	**66,286**

Chart adapted from Cowe, AVNT, 256.

*Many of these languages are not cataloged regularly.
**25,000 are relatively recent, dated to the nineteenth and twentieth centuries.

It can be hard to grasp the meaning of these numbers on their own, so let's compare the New Testament with other ancient documents.

Comparison with Surviving Manuscript Copies of Selected Classical Literature

Here is a table providing the number of manuscripts and dates of various writings of antiquity:

SUMMARY CHART OF SELECTED SURVIVING MSS OF MAJOR CLASSICAL WORKS

Work	Earliest MS (old)	Earliest MS (new)	Number of MSS (old)	Number of MSS (new)
Homer's *Iliad*	About 400 BC	About 415 BC	1,800+	1,900+
Herodotus's *Histories*	1st c. AD	150–50 BC	109	About 106

Work	Earliest MS (old)	Earliest MS (new)	Number of MSS (old)	Number of MSS (new)
Sophocles's plays	3rd c. BC	3rd c. BC	193	About 226
Plato's tetralogies	AD 895	3rd c. BC	210	238
Caesar's *Gallic Wars*	9th c. AD	9th c. AD	251	251
Livy's *History of Rome*	Early 5th c. AD	4th c. AD	150	About 473
Tacitus's *Annals*	1st half: AD 850 2nd half: AD 1050	1st half: AD 850 2nd half: AD 1050	33	36
Pliny the Elder's *Natural History*	One 5th c. AD fragment. Others in 14th and 15th c.	5th c. AD	200	200+
Thucydides's *History*	3rd c. BC	3rd c. BC	96	188
Demosthenes's speeches	Fragments from 1st c. BC	1st c. BC, possibly earlier	340	444
TOTAL				4,062+

As the table clearly shows, the New Testament is in a category of its own. There is no other work of antiquity that has more and earlier copies than the New Testament. Thus, we are on solid ground to conclude that the text of the New Testament meets the bibliographical test. Let's now turn to the second test.

INTERNAL EVIDENCE TEST

For the internal evidence test, we ask the question, Does the document have internal signs of being reliable? One way to undermine the testimony of a document is to show that it is full of contradictions. Is this true for the New Testament?

Objection: The Bible Is Full of Contradictions

A common objection to the reliability of the Bible is that it is full of contradictions. While some statements may appear contradictory, many apparent contradictions can be resolved with just a little research. For example, the Gospels and Acts provide conflicting versions of the death of Judas Iscariot. Matthew relates that Judas died by hanging himself. But Acts says that Judas fell headlong into a field, and "he burst open in the middle and all his entrails gushed out" (Acts 1:18). How can both be true? Easy. Judas hung himself, but the branch or the rope broke and his body fell into a field. This explanation is not a desperate attempt at harmonization but is suggested by the text itself. When a living person falls, he does not generally burst open. But if Judas were already dead, and it was his body that fell from some height, this is what we might expect. The cliffs overlooking the Valley of Hinnom could be the place where Judas hanged himself and his body fell and burst open.

While we can't address every alleged contradiction in the Bible, we have consistently found that when the genre, context, and cultural background are taken into consideration, alleged contradictions have plausible explanations. It is important to calibrate our expectations to other writings of the time. Interestingly, we find plenty of examples of variations and discrepancies in other ancient texts, such as the various accounts of the assassination of Julius Caesar. Further, variations in testimony may also indicate that writings are sources independent of one another.

Reliable Testimony

Fairy tales often begin "Once upon a time." The opening of the movies of the Star Wars saga reads "A long time ago in a galaxy far, far away." Such stories bear the markings of make-believe. But not the Bible. The writers of the New Testament wrote as eyewitnesses or from reliable testimony, and they wanted their readers to know it. Consider the way Luke opens his gospel.

> Inasmuch as many have taken in hand to set in order a narrative of those things which have been fulfilled among us, just as those who from the beginning were eyewitnesses and ministers of the word delivered them to us, it seemed good to me also, having had perfect understanding of all things from the very first, to write to you an orderly account, most excellent Theophilus. (Luke 1:1–3)

Luke wants his readers to know they are reading true, reliable accounts. The New Testament writers consistently claim to be reporting reliable testimony to the events they describe (2 Pet. 1:16; 1 John 1:3; Acts 2:32; John 19:35).

Does this sound like fiction to you? No. The biblical authors wanted their readers to know they were writing history.

Embarrassing Details

If you were writing a story about your life, would you include embarrassing stories or details that showed you in a negative light? Probably not. But the New Testament includes many things that could be considered embarrassing and even harmful to the leaders of the Christian movement. For example, Jesus's family, including his brother James, thought he was crazy (Mark 3:21; John 7:5). The disciples are repeatedly portrayed as being doubtful (Matt. 28:17), dim-witted and slow to understand Jesus's teachings (Mark 8:14–21, 31–33; 9:31–32; 10:35–40), cowards (John 20:19), and even deniers of Jesus (John 18:25–26). Why would the New Testament writers include these details if they weren't true?

Let's turn to the third and final test for the reliability of historical documents.

EXTERNAL EVIDENCE TEST

Is there any evidence *outside* of the Bible to corroborate the contents *inside* the Bible? Yes, there is. We've devoted an entire chapter to the archaeological evidence for the Gospels (chapter 16) to show that the New Testament is historically accurate. To show that the New Testament has been transmitted accurately over time, we can refer to what cold-case detective J. Warner Wallace calls the "chain of custody."[1] To ensure that a piece of evidence has not been tampered with over time, there must be a trail of records for every time the evidence has been handled or passed to someone else. Like a piece of evidence from a crime scene, the New Testament has followed a careful "chain of custody."

Following the Great Commission, Jesus's disciples made disciples, and those disciples made disciples, and so on. For example, two of the apostle John's disciples were the church fathers Ignatius and Polycarp. Those men passed on what they learned, citing the gospels in their writings and providing teachings that were consistent with the Bible. Their student Irenaeus passed on their teaching to Hippolytus, and so on. Thus, we have a consistent chain of custody of the New Testament writings and teachings that continues throughout the centuries since the events of Jesus's life.

As we explored in chapter 2, there are also extrabiblical writings that corroborate key events in Jesus's life, such as his crucifixion by the Romans and James being his brother.

Thus, we can see that the New Testament passes the third and final test for the reliability for historical documents.

CONCLUSION

Much more could be said in defense of the reliability of the New Testament. And there are other objections to consider as well. But this should be enough to show that we have good reason to trust the New Testament documents as reliable.

CONCLUSION

BOTH CHRISTIAN AND SECULAR SCHOLARS FROM A VARIETY of theological traditions have concluded that there is enough evidence to confidently affirm that Jesus truly existed. Bart Ehrman, for example, is extremely skeptical about many things that conservative Christian scholars affirm. But even he sees overwhelming evidence that a man named Jesus who served as the foundation of the Christian faith actually lived in ancient Israel:

> The reality is that every single author who mentions Jesus—pagan, Christian, or Jewish—was fully convinced that he at least lived. Even the enemies of the Jesus movement thought so; among their many slurs against the religion, his nonexistence is never one of them. . . . Jesus certainly existed.[1]

While we differ with Ehrman on many of his claims about the New Testament, we concur wholeheartedly with his conclusions about the existence of Jesus. The weight of evidence, including the New Testament as well as Christian *and* non-Christian extrabiblical sources, is too strong for reasonable doubt that Jesus was a historical person.

THE IDENTITY OF JESUS

WHEN I (JOSH) SET OUT TO INVESTIGATE THE IDENTITY OF Jesus, I soon realized that Christianity was uniquely based on the idea that Jesus is the eternal creator who took on human flesh. No other religious figure has made such an audacious claim. Moses didn't. Krishna didn't. Muhammad didn't. Buddha didn't. Among all the great religious leaders, Jesus uniquely claimed to be God in human flesh. Unsurprisingly, skeptics contest such a claim. What does the evidence suggest regarding Jesus's identity?

CHAPTER 5

DID JESUS CLAIM TO BE GOD?

CRITICS OF CHRISTIANITY ARGUE THAT JESUS NEVER uttered the words, "I am God." Technically, they're right! But while Jesus is not recorded in the Bible as ever having said those three words, that doesn't mean Jesus did not claim deity. Let's explore a few key ways that Jesus made divine claims.

During Jesus's trial, the high priest asked him, "Are You the Christ, the Son of the Blessed?" Jesus responded, "I am. And you will see the Son of Man sitting at the right hand of the Power, and coming with the clouds of heaven" (Mark 14:62). This infuriated the high priest, and Jesus was condemned to death.

The first two words of Jesus's response were enough to establish his deity. But what is significant about the words that follow, about the term "Son of Man"? Jesus was alluding to Daniel's vision of one "coming with the clouds of heaven" and given an everlasting kingdom over "all peoples, nations, and languages." On trial for his life, he was addressing Jewish scholars who would recognize his response as an electrifying claim from Daniel 7:13–14.

Jesus clearly made lofty, seemingly audacious self-proclamations at his trial. Was this an isolated occurrence or indicative of a broader pattern of statements and behavior?

We must look at Jesus's other claims that ultimately led to his arrest and trial. On several occasions, Jesus claimed to be equal to God the Father. Here's a selection of relevant passages:

JESUS'S CLAIMS OF DIVINITY

John 10:25, 30–33

Jesus answered . . . "I and the Father are one."

The Jews picked up stones again to stone him. Jesus answered them, "I have shown you many good works from the Father; for which of them are you going to stone me?" The Jews answered him, "It is not for a good work that we are going to stone you but for blasphemy, because you, being a man, make yourself God." (ESV)

Just as in the account of Jesus's trial, the response of his audience in John 10 demonstrates the gravity of his words. There was no doubt in their minds that Jesus's claim to be one with the Father was an assertion of deity.

John 5:17–18

Jesus answered them, "My Father has been working until now, and I have been working."

Therefore the Jews sought all the more to kill Him, because He not only broke the Sabbath, but also said that God was His Father, making Himself equal with God.

In this exchange, Jesus's hearers again interpret his statement to be a declaration of parity with God.

John 8:57–59

> Then the Jews said to Him, "You are not yet fifty years old, and have You seen Abraham?"
>
> Jesus said to them, "Most assuredly, I say to you, before Abraham was, I AM."
>
> Then they took up stones to throw at Him.

The phrase "I AM" is broadly understood to refer to the God of the Old Testament and was so understood by Jesus's Jewish audience. (Their response indicates their instant recognition that such a statement made by a mere man would be blasphemy, deserving death.) For example, in the book of Exodus, God said to Moses, "I AM WHO I AM. . . . Thus you shall say to the children of Israel, 'I AM has sent me to you'" (Ex. 3:14).

Moreover, Jesus's Jewish audience questions him about his claim to have known the patriarch Abraham. In response, Jesus implies his own preexistence, saying, "Most assuredly, I say to you, before Abraham was, I AM" (John 8:58).

As we observed in each of the prior scriptural passages examined, the reaction of Jesus's audience leaves little doubt that they understood his reference as a claim to divinity. They quickly set about to administering the Mosaic Law's penalty for blasphemy by attempting to stone him.

John 5:22–23

> "The Father judges no one, but has given all judgment to the Son, that all may honor the Son, just as they honor the Father. Whoever does not honor the Son does not honor the Father who sent him." (ESV)

We already considered John 5:17–18, when Jesus portrayed himself as equal with God. In these verses, Jesus elaborates on that theme with two profound statements: First, he claims to be worthy of the same honor due God the Father. Second, he declares that God cannot be honored unless Jesus himself is also honored.

John 14:7–9

"If you had known me, you would have known my Father also. From now on you do know him and have seen him."

Philip said to him, "Lord, show us the Father, and it is enough for us." Jesus said to him, "Have I been with you so long, and you still do not know me, Philip? Whoever has seen me has seen the Father. How can you say, 'Show us the Father'?" (ESV)

Jesus declares that to know and see him is equivalent to knowing and seeing the Father.

Matthew 11:27

"All things have been handed over to me by my Father, and no one knows the Son except the Father, and no one knows the Father except the Son and anyone to whom the Son chooses to reveal him." (ESV)

The first part of this statement appears ordinary. When Jesus says that "no one knows the Son except the Father," he seems simply to observe about himself what many others might likewise observe: that God's knowledge of him is exceptional. However, when he continues, saying that his own knowledge of God the Father is reciprocally exceptional, he makes a remarkable claim of equality with God. The gospel of Luke records a similar account, but its placement here, in Matthew, reinforces that statements like these by Jesus are attested outside the gospel of John.

Matthew 5:21–22

> You have heard that it was said to those of old . . . But I say to you . . .

This statement is an excerpt from Jesus's Sermon on the Mount, where he repeatedly cites the Old Testament law and then asserts his own authority as supreme. This was extraordinary in a Jewish culture that revered the teachings of its prophets and patriarchs as sacred. Instead of repeating the prophets by saying, "Thus saith the Lord," Jesus elevates the authority of his own words above theirs. On at least six occasions (commonly referred to as the antitheses), he uses the formula, "You have heard that it was said . . . but I say to you." For example, Jesus recites the commands against murder and adultery, then declares that the essence of those mandates is directed at an individual's thought life (Matt. 5:21–30), something the Mosaic law does not explicitly broach. He later appears to undermine the Mosaic system of vows and oaths, stating, "Do not take an oath at all. . . . Let what you say be simply 'Yes' or 'No'; anything more than this comes from evil" (Matt. 5:34, 37 ESV). In these sayings of Jesus, he claims an authority superior to that of both Jewish tradition and the Mosaic law.

RECEIVING WORSHIP

Another way that Jesus claimed to be God is by receiving worship. Why is this significant? The Bible issues a persistent warning against worshiping anything or anyone but God himself. In Matthew 4:10, Jesus himself says, "You shall worship the LORD your God, and Him only you shall serve." The first of the Ten Commandments states, "You shall have no other gods before Me" (Ex. 20:3). The Old Testament is filled with cautions against idolatry, admonitions to those engaging in the practice, warnings of grave consequences should they persist, and detailed descriptions of those consequences as they were experienced. The New Testament similarly warns people to "flee from idolatry" (1 Cor. 10:14).

Jesus's disciples understood this message. Peter rejects worship in Acts 10:25–26, and Paul and Barnabas reject worship in Acts 14:11–15. Worship is inappropriate even for elevated spiritual beings, such as angels. In the book of Revelation, the apostle John falls at the feet of an angel to worship him, but the angel admonishes him (Rev. 19:10).

Yet we find that Jesus accepted worship. Note the examples in Matthew 14:33, John 9:38, Matthew 28:9, and Luke 24:52. When one reads the full context of these passages, Jesus never corrects people for worshiping him. In particular, the religious context of Luke 24:52, which occurs after Jesus's ascension into heaven, clearly indicates that the disciples worshiped him. In contrast to his disciples and angels, Jesus readily accepted worship.

Not only did Jesus accept worship during his first-century ministry, but the New Testament alludes to current and future worship of Jesus. For example, the book of Hebrews says, "Let all the angels of God worship [Jesus]" (Heb. 1:6). The book of Revelation likewise describes the future worship of Jesus: "And the twenty-four elders fell down and worshiped [Jesus]" (Rev. 5:14).

CONCLUSION

The Gospels record many examples of Jesus claiming to be God. But what did those closest to Jesus think of him? Let's turn to that next.

CHAPTER 6

WHAT DID THE FOLLOWERS OF JESUS THINK ABOUT HIS IDENTITY?

A NUMBER OF YEARS AGO, I (SEAN) WAS STUDYING IN A coffee shop when a lady sat down next to me and started reading a book by a prominent atheist. When I leaned forward and asked her what she thought of the book, she lit up with how meaningful she found it. To follow up, I asked her what it said about Jesus. As best as I can remember, here's what she said: "Jesus was not the Son of God. He was not born of a virgin. He was just a really nice guy. The church has gotten it wrong." All I could think of was to ask a simple question: "If Jesus was just a nice guy, why did they kill him?" Think about it: If Jesus was just a nice guy, why torture him to death?

Jesus was put to death not for what he did but for who he claimed to be. As we saw in the last chapter, Jesus made claims to be divine. As we will see in this chapter, his closest followers also believed that Jesus was God. While the apostle Paul was not one of his twelve disciples, he saw the risen Jesus and became the greatest missionary ever.

THE APOSTLE PAUL

Before we consider some specific examples of Paul affirming the deity of Jesus, it is important to note that Paul emphasized strongly that he preached the same gospel as the apostles. He portrayed himself as being on the same team as Cephas [Peter] and Apollos (1 Cor. 1:12–13), and he confirmed that his gospel message was the same as that of the apostles when he visited Jerusalem (Gal. 2:6). The book of Acts, written by a traveling companion of Paul who wrote careful historical accounts, also confirms that the message of Paul aligned with the rest of the apostles.

Why is this important? If Paul agreed with the other apostles on the core tenets of the gospel, including the deity of Christ (as we will see), this suggests that he and the apostles—that is, those who knew Jesus personally during his earthly ministry—shared a view about the identity of Jesus.

Romans 9:5

> To them belong the patriarchs, and from their race, according to the flesh, is the Christ, who is God over all, blessed forever. Amen. (ESV)

In Romans 9:1–5, Paul begins with a yearning for Israel to come to know Christ and ends by proclaiming that Jesus is "God over all."

Philippians 2:6–11

> [Jesus,] who, being in very nature God,
> did not consider equality with God something
> to be used to his own advantage;

rather, he made himself nothing
>   by taking the very nature of a servant,
>   being made in human likeness.
And being found in appearance as a man,
>   he humbled himself
>   by becoming obedient to death—
>   even death on a cross!

Therefore God exalted him to the highest place
>   and gave him the name that is above
>   every name,
that at the name of Jesus every knee
>   should bow,
>   in heaven and on earth and under the earth,
and every tongue acknowledge that Jesus
>   Christ is Lord,
>   to the glory of God the Father. (NIV)

This passage begins with the apostle Paul describing Christ as having preexisted as God before voluntarily taking on human likeness. Paul also describes Jesus as having taken on a dual nature, being both truly God and truly man. He expresses this by affirming that Jesus possessed both the "nature" of God (v. 6) and the "nature" of a human servant (v. 7). Paul says that after Jesus's death, he was again exalted to the highest place, to which "every knee should bow" (v. 10).

Thus, Paul here confesses the deity of Christ in three ways: by his preexistent God nature, by his dual nature as both human and divine, and by ultimately equating him with the exclusive name of God (Lord, Yahweh) of the Old Testament.

Colossians 1:15–17

[Jesus] is the image of the invisible God, the firstborn of all creation. For by him all things were created, in heaven and on earth, visible and invisible, whether thrones or dominions or rulers or authorities—all things were created through him and for him. And he is before all things, and in him all things hold together. (ESV)

The apostle Paul again ascribes attributes of deity to Jesus, whom he refers to as "the image of the invisible God" (v. 15). He asserts that even though God the Father is unseen, his image and likeness have been conveyed through Jesus. Paul then credits Jesus with a central role in creation, stating that all things were created by him, through him, and for him.

Colossians 2:9

For in [Jesus] dwells all the fullness of the Godhead bodily.

This is perhaps the most succinct statement of the understanding of Jesus held by the apostle Paul and his contemporaries.

Titus 2:13

Waiting for our blessed hope, the appearing of the glory of our great God and Savior Jesus Christ. (ESV)

By referring to Jesus as "our great God and Savior," Paul clearly declares Jesus to be God.

While Paul offers the most direct statements of Jesus being God, references to Jesus's deity are also made by plenty of others in the New Testament.

JOHN THE BAPTIST

John 1:29, 34

> The next day he saw Jesus coming toward him, and said, "Behold, the Lamb of God, who takes away the sin of the world! . . . And I have seen and have borne witness that this is the Son of God." (ESV)

In this passage, John the Baptist bears witness that he has personally seen Jesus, the Son of God, who will bring forgiveness to the world. The next chapter elaborates on the uniqueness of Jesus's sonship and why the title "Son of God" in this context refers to his deity.

THE APOSTLE PETER

2 Peter 1:1

> Simon Peter, a servant and apostle of Jesus Christ,
> To those who through the righteousness of our God and Savior Jesus Christ have received a faith as precious as ours. (NIV)

Peter echoes the expression Paul uses in Titus 2:13, calling Jesus "our God and Savior." This was a common first-century religious expression referring to Yahweh, and so this title affirms that both Paul and Peter believed Jesus was God.

THE APOSTLE THOMAS

John 20:28

> Thomas answered and said to Him, "My Lord and my God!"

We noted in the previous chapter that Jesus's acceptance of worship was evidence of his claim to deity. After Jesus appears to Thomas, inviting him to touch his hands and his side, Thomas worships Jesus as God.

THE WRITER OF HEBREWS

Hebrews 1:3

> [Jesus] is the radiance of the glory of God and the exact imprint of his nature, and he upholds the universe by the word of his power. (ESV)

Jesus is said not merely to be like God in some way but rather is the "exact imprint of his nature."

Hebrews 1:6

> And again, when he brings the firstborn into the world, he says,

> > "Let all God's angels worship him." (ESV)

In this passage, the author of Hebrews quotes the LXX of Deuteronomy 32:43, which is a longer version not found in the standard Hebrew text. The point is that Jesus is the firstborn who is superior to angels and worthy of their worship, as is the Father.

THE APOSTLE JOHN

John 1:1, 14

> In the beginning was the Word, and the Word was with God, and the Word was God. . . . And the Word became flesh and dwelt among us, and we beheld His glory, the glory as of the only begotten of the Father, full of grace and truth.

This passage teaches that the Word (Jesus) was eternal alongside God, was God, and yet was distinct from the Father. In verse 14, John says, "We beheld His glory." This alludes to Isaiah 40:5, which mentions the glory of the Lord being revealed. By making this allusion between the glory of God and Jesus, John represents Jesus as God in human flesh.

1 John 5:20

> We know that the Son of God has come and has given us understanding, so that we may know him who is true; and we are in him who is true, in his Son Jesus Christ. He is the true God and eternal life. (ESV)

With the final statement, "He is the true God and eternal life," the apostle John again declares Jesus to be both the Son of God and God.

CONCLUSION

We learned in chapter 5 that Jesus had a divine self-understanding. In this chapter, we have seen that his closest friends and first followers also believed Jesus was God. They refered to him as the Son of God and "God over all," and they worshiped him as divine. As seen through both their words and actions, the first followers of Jesus truly believed he was God in human flesh. They believed this so deeply, they suffered and died for this belief (for more on this, see chapter 25). In the next chapter, we'll examine the indirect evidence that Jesus is God.

CHAPTER 7

IS THERE CIRCUMSTANTIAL EVIDENCE THAT JESUS IS GOD?

WHEN I (JOSH) BEGAN INVESTIGATING THE HISTORICAL Jesus, I wanted to know not only if he had a divine self-understanding but also if he acted in a manner consistent with that belief. In other words, do his actions back up his claims? It turns out that they do. Jesus acted as if he had divine authority rooted in his unique identity as the Son of God. While these are not overt claims to be God, these pieces of circumstantial evidence contribute to a cumulative case regarding Jesus's divine identity. Simply put, he lived his life as if he believed he was divine. Let's consider a few examples of how his actions support his divine claims.

JESUS FORGAVE SINS

Mark 2:5–7 says, "When Jesus saw their faith, he said to the paralytic, 'Son, your sins are forgiven.' Now some of the scribes were sitting there, questioning in their hearts, 'Why does this man speak like that? He is blaspheming! Who can forgive sins but God alone?'" (ESV).

To the Jewish scribes steeped in the law of God, it was

inconceivable that a man could forgive sins committed against God. Forgiveness, in that sense, was a prerogative of God alone. Although Jesus did not claim to be God in Mark 2, not only his actions reveal a person with godlike authority, but the responses of the people infer this as well.

Some of Jesus's critics questioned whether he had the divine authority to forgive sins. He knew his audience had doubts about this, so he demonstrated his authority to them:

> "Which is easier, to say to the paralytic, 'Your sins are forgiven,' or to say, 'Rise, take up your bed and walk'? But that you may know that the Son of Man has authority on earth to forgive sins"—he said to the paralytic—"I say to you, rise, pick up your bed, and go home." And he rose and immediately picked up his bed and went out before them all, so that they were all amazed and glorified God, saying, "We never saw anything like this!" (Mark 2:9–12 ESV)

JESUS CLAIMED TO BE "LIFE"

In John 14:6 Jesus stated, "I am the way, the truth, and the life." Jesus did not say he knew or was teaching the way, the truth, and the life. He claimed he *is* the way, the truth, and the life. He was not creating a new religious system; he himself was the path to salvation.

JESUS HAS AUTHORITY

The Old Testament teaches that God is the judge over all of creation (Gen. 18:25; Ps. 50:4–6; 96:13). That God is judge is not disputed. Yet the New Testament reveals that Jesus possesses this divine authority, fulfilling the vision of Daniel 7:13–14. Jesus, speaking of himself in the third person as the Son of Man, claimed this authority. For example, in John 5:22 and 5:27 Jesus himself made this claim even when facing those who wanted to kill him (John 5:18), declaring that the Father "has given all judgment to the Son. . . . And he has given [Jesus] authority to execute judgment, because he is the Son of Man" (ESV). Later, Jesus prayed, "Father, the hour has come; glorify your Son that the Son may glorify you, since you have given him authority over all flesh" (John 17:1–2 ESV).

At the conclusion of the gospel of Matthew, Jesus gathers a group of his disciples to a mountain in Galilee for some final words, a moment later called the Great Commission. He begins his directives to them with the forceful declaration, "All authority in heaven and on earth has been given to me" (Matt. 28:18 ESV). By claiming all authority, Jesus means he shares God's throne, which positions him over the entire universe.

JESUS PREEXISTED

The New Testament makes another noteworthy claim: that Jesus existed before his life on earth. At one time he prayed, "And now, O Father, glorify Me together with Yourself, with the glory which I had with You before the world was" (John 17:5). He also taught people, "I have come down from heaven, not to do My own will, but the will of Him who sent Me" (John 6:38). Many similar statements are found throughout the Gospels and in the New Testament Epistles (for example,

Phil. 2:6–11; John 3:13; 6:33, 62; 8:23, 58; 16:28; Rom. 8:3; 1 John 1:2; and Gal. 4:4).

TITLES OF DEITY

Another way that Jesus is indirectly alluded to as God is through divine titles. The New Testament authors ascribed to Jesus many of the titles used for God in the Old Testament, thus showing that they believed Jesus was the very same God of the Old Testament.

JESUS IS DECLARED TO BE JEHOVAH GOD[*]

Said of Jehovah	Mutual Title or Act	Said of Jesus
Gen. 1:1–3; Ps. 102:25; Isa. 44:24	Creator	John 1:3; Heb. 1:2
Isa. 45:15, 21–22; 43:11	Savior	John 4:42
Deut. 32:39; 1 Sam. 2:6	Raising the Dead	John 5:28, 29
Ps. 62:12; Joel 3:12	Judge	Matt. 25:31–46; John 5:22
Isa. 60:19–20	Light	John 8:12
Ex. 3:14	I Am	John 8:58
Ps. 23:1	Shepherd	John 10:11
Isa. 42:8; cf. 48:11	Glory of God	John 17:1, 5

(continued)

Said of Jehovah	Mutual Title or Act	Said of Jesus
Isa. 41:4; 44:6; 48:12	First and Last	Rev. 1:7–8, 17–18; 2:8; 22:12–13
Hos. 13:14	Redeemer	Rev. 5:9
Isa. 62:5; Hos. 2:16	Bridegroom	Rev. 21:2
Ps. 18:2	Rock	1 Cor. 10:4
Ex. 34:6–7; Jer. 31:34	Forgiver of Sins	Mark 2:7–10; Acts 5:31
Ps. 97:7; 148:2	Worshiped by Angels	Heb. 1:6
Joel 2:32; throughout OT	Addressed in Prayer	Acts 7:59–60; Rom. 10:12–13
Ps. 148:2–5	Creator of Angels	Col. 1:16
Isa. 45:23	Confessed as Lord (Jehovah)	Phil. 2:9–11

*This chart originally appeared in Josh McDowell, *The New Evidence That Demands a Verdict* (Nashville, TN: Thomas Nelson, 1999), 148.

YHWH (Lord)

Many English Bibles translate the Old Testament name of God as "Lord" or "Jehovah." The word in the original Hebrew is made up of four consonants: YHWH. Many transliterate this Hebrew word as "Jehovah," but a closer phonetic rendering in English of the Hebrew consonants is probably "Yahweh." According to tradition, the Jewish people have regarded this name as unutterable, as most sacred.

Given the Jewish reverence for the name of God, it is especially striking that the title is applied to Jesus in the New Testament. For example,

- Psalm 102:25–27 (LXX vv. 26–28; cf. Ps. 102:22 for YHWH) and Hebrews 1:10–12
- Isaiah 45:24–25 and Philippians 2:10–11

Son of God

Perhaps the best-known title ascribed to Jesus is Son of God. It is found throughout each of the four gospels and other New Testament books. In the gospel of Matthew, the disciples worship Jesus as the Son of God (14:33). In the climax of the gospel, Jesus identifies himself as the "Christ, the Son of God" (Matthew 26:63–64). Matthew also quotes Jesus's exclusive claim, "All things have been handed over to me by my Father, and no one knows the Son except the Father, and no one knows the Father except the Son and anyone to whom the Son chooses to reveal him" (Matt. 11:27 ESV).

John repeatedly uses the phrase *only begotten* to convey the uniqueness of Jesus's sonship. This is exemplified in John 3:16, which states, "For God so loved the world that He gave His only begotten Son, that whoever believes in Him should not perish but have everlasting life." The first chapter of John similarly declares, "We beheld His glory, the glory as of the only begotten of the Father" (John 1:14).

Son of Man

Earlier in this book, we noted the implications of Jesus's "Son of Man" statement during his trial before the Sanhedrin. There, he makes a clear reference to the Son of Man in Daniel 7:13 as an indication of his deity. The following is a further elaboration of the three primary ways in which Jesus utilized the phrase *Son of Man*.

Concerning His Earthly Ministry

Jesus used the term *Son of Man* when speaking of his earthly ministry, linking this exalted name to his identification with poor and lost people, his having come with godly power to bring salvation, and his taking upon himself the death that humans deserved (Matt. 8:20; 9:6; 11:19; Luke 19:10; 22:48).

When Foretelling His Passion

Jesus used the term *Son of Man* when warning his disciples of his death and connecting it with the Old Testament Scriptures (Matt. 12:40; 17:9, 22; 20:18).

In His Teaching Regarding His Coming Again

Jesus appropriately used the term *Son of Man* when he taught about his coming again as the glorious judge of all humanity, as Daniel had prophesied (Matt. 13:41; 24:27, 30; 25:31; Luke 18:8; 21:36).

Abba (Father)

In using the Aramaic word *Abba*, a word of close intimacy, Jesus described a relationship with God that no one else had (Mark 14:36). Nowhere in the Old Testament does this kind of familiarity with God appear. Not even King David, who wrote most of the psalms and was known for his closeness to God, prayed in such intimate terms.

The Pharisees realized the implications of the language Jesus used. As the gospel of John states, "This was why the Jews were seeking all the more to kill him, because not only was he breaking the Sabbath, but he was even calling God his own Father, making himself equal with God" (5:18 ESV).

CONCLUSION

Even if Jesus never explicitly stated that he is God, he certainly made many implicit and indirect claims to deity. Jesus forgave sins and accepted worship. He claimed a special relationship with the Father and referred to himself using titles explicitly reserved for God. Thus, we have collected plenty of evidence in this and the previous two chapters to demonstrate that Jesus and his closest friends and followers believed he was God in the flesh.

But still, what if they were wrong? What if Jesus simply fooled everyone to gain attention for himself or suffered from a serious delusion? This is the subject of our next chapter.

CHAPTER 8

WAS JESUS MERELY A PROPHET OR A GOOD PERSON?

ONCE I (JOSH) CONCLUDED THAT JESUS CLAIMED TO BE GOD, I realized I only had so many options left. I could reject this claim, which would mean that Jesus was either a liar who knew he wasn't God but said so anyway or a lunatic who believed he was God but wasn't. Or I could accept this claim, which, for me, would mean becoming a Christian. This has famously been called the "liar, lunatic, Lord" trilemma. In his classic book *Mere Christianity*, Oxford literary scholar C. S. Lewis explained why he rejected two of these options:

> I am trying here to prevent anyone saying the really foolish thing that people often say about Him: "I'm ready to accept Jesus as a great moral teacher, but I don't accept His claim to be God." That is the one thing we must not say. A man who was merely a man and said the sort of things Jesus said would not be a great moral teacher. He would either be a lunatic—on a level with the man who says he is a poached egg—or else he would be the Devil of Hell. You must make your choice. Either this man was, and is, the Son of God: or else a madman or something

worse. You can shut Him up for a fool, you can spit at Him and kill Him as a demon; or you can fall at His feet and call Him Lord and God. But let us not come with any patronising nonsense about His being a great human teacher. He has not left that open to us. He did not intend to.[1]

In the first century, when people were giving several answers about Jesus's identity, Jesus asked his disciples, "Who do you say that I am?" to which Peter responded, "You are the Christ, the Son of the living God" (Matt. 16:15–16). Not everyone accepts Peter's answer, but no one should avoid Jesus's question. Jesus's claim to be God must be either true or false. If Jesus's claims were true, then he is the Lord, which we must either accept or reject. But if Jesus's claims to be God were false, then we are left with just two options: he either knew his claims were false (he was a liar), or he did not know they were false (he was crazy). We will consider each alternative separately and the evidence for each.

JESUS WAS A LIAR

If Jesus knew he was not God, then he was lying. That would also make him a hypocrite since he told others to be honest, whatever the cost. More than that, he would have been a demon, because he deliberately told others to forsake their own religious beliefs and trust him for their eternal destiny. If Jesus knew his claims to be false, we would have to conclude that he was unspeakably evil. The religious leaders did charge Jesus with having a demon (John 8:48). But the gospel of John makes it clear Jesus believed he was telling the truth (John 8:45–46). Last, if Jesus had been lying, he would also have been a fool because his claims to deity led to his crucifixion.

> He remained silent and made no answer. Again the high priest asked him, "Are you the Christ, the Son of the Blessed?" And Jesus said, "I am, and you will see the Son of Man seated at the right hand of Power, and coming with the clouds of heaven." And the high priest tore his garments and said, "What further witnesses do we need? You have heard his blasphemy. What is your decision?" And they all condemned him as deserving death. (Mark 14:61–64 ESV)

> The Jews answered him, "We have a law, and according to that law he ought to die because he has made himself the Son of God." (John 19:7 ESV)

But how could Jesus—as liar, con man, evil, foolish—leave us with the most profound moral instruction and the most powerful moral example in history? Could a deceiver—an imposter of monstrous proportions—teach such unselfish ethical truths and live such a morally exemplary life as Jesus did? The very notion is incredible.

In his book *Cold-Case Christianity*, cold-case homicide detective J. Warner Wallace lists the three types of motives that lie at the heart of any misbehavior: (1) financial greed, (2) sexual or relational desire, and (3) pursuit of power. Is there good reason to suspect Jesus was led to lie by any of these three motives?

+ **Financial greed.** Jesus is never described as a man who possessed financial wealth. He taught his disciples to give their possessions to the needy and not to store up treasure in this life but to store up spiritual treasure in the life to come (Luke 12:32–34). He told the rich young ruler, "If you want to be perfect, go, sell what you have and give to the poor, and you will have treasure in heaven; and come, follow Me" (Matt. 19:21). Jesus gained nothing financially from his preaching, teaching, or healing ministry.

+ **Sexual or relational desire.** No evidence suggests that Jesus was motivated by lust or relationships. Many women followed Jesus (Luke 8:1–3), many of them coming from vulnerable situations. He could have taken advantage of them, as other men in positions of power have done. But by all accounts, Jesus showed women the highest respect, even in ways that were countercultural at the time (see Luke 8:42–48; John 4:1–45).

+ **The pursuit of power.** It is utterly unreasonable to assert that Jesus lied about his identity to gain power. Rather than gaining power for himself, he modeled serving others (John 13:1–16; 15:13) and giving without expectation of return, even to the wicked and ungrateful (Luke 6:35–36), and he taught his disciples to do the same. In a dispute over who would be greatest in the kingdom, Jesus taught his disciples that the greatest is the one who serves (Luke 22:24–27).

With what we know from Scripture, Jesus was not motivated to lie about his identity for any reason. Was he crazy?

JESUS WAS CRAZY

It is inconceivable for Jesus to have been a liar, but perhaps he *thought* he was God but was mistaken. After all, one can be both sincere and sincerely wrong. We must remember, though, that for someone to think he was God, especially in a fiercely monotheistic culture—and to tell others that their eternal destiny depended on believing in him—was no slight flight of fantasy. These were the thoughts of a lunatic in the fullest sense. Further, the number of individuals who truly believe they are God is extremely small. Apart from the following considerations, the probability that Jesus is among this class is already quite small. Was Jesus such a person?

Reading the Gospels, we see a man of great wisdom, compassion, and wonder. Jesus constantly outwitted the religious leaders when they sought to entrap him. He loved and served even the most marginalized and unloved people of his time. Jesus constantly amazed people with his teachings and authority. He also had incredible insight into the human mind and heart. There is no reason to believe Jesus was crazy. Jesus was no lunatic.

In light of what we know about Jesus and his impact, it is difficult to conclude that he was mentally disturbed. He spoke some of the most profound words ever spoken. He told some of the most memorable stories ever told. His instructions have liberated countless people in mental bondage. Professor Clark Pinnock concludes, "Was he deluded about his greatness, a paranoid, an unintentional deceiver, a schizophrenic? Again, the skill and depth of his teaching support the case only for his total mental soundness. If only we were as sane as he!"[2]

JESUS IS LORD

If Jesus of Nazareth is not a liar or a lunatic, then he must be Lord. Jesus's closest friends and followers believed him to be God, as did the writers of the New Testament. Here are some examples of people in the Bible explicitly proclaiming Jesus to be God:

- Peter (Matt. 16:16)
- Martha (John 11:27)
- Thomas (John 20:28)
- Mark (Mark 1:1)
- John (John 20:31)
- The author of Hebrews (Heb. 1:3)

So while Jesus may never have outright proclaimed to be God, many people from his lifetime believed Jesus was God in the flesh. Additionally, it seems quite unlikely that so many of Jesus's immediate followers would have come to believe he was God incarnate, given their Jewish background and the fact that Jesus endured the shameful death of crucifixion, unless Jesus had made this claim about himself.

CONCLUSION

Answering the question, Who is Jesus of Nazareth? cannot be an idle intellectual exercise. Jesus cannot be put on the shelf as a great moral teacher. He is either a liar, a lunatic, or the Lord. You must choose. As the apostle John wrote, "These are written so that you may believe that Jesus is the Christ, the Son of God, and that by believing you may have life in his name" (John 20:31 ESV).

The evidence favors Jesus as Lord. However, some people reject the clear evidence because of the moral implications involved. This moral dilemma is the true reason many people resist, not the academic dilemma. If Jesus is Lord, people are obligated to follow him or else honestly reject him and be held responsible accordingly. Therein lies the greatest challenge. There needs to be moral honesty in the consideration of Jesus as either liar, lunatic, or Lord and God.

SECTION 2

CONCLUSION

THIS SECTION ASKED THE QUESTION, WHO IS JESUS OF Nazareth? The New Testament consistently represents him making direct claims to deity. Jesus claimed to be equal with God the Father and worthy of commensurate honor. He said that seeing and knowing him was the same as seeing and knowing the Father. He claimed the unique characteristics of God, such as sovereignty, judgment, divine authority, forgiveness of sins, and preexistence. These assertions—corroborated by the doctrine of Jesus's eyewitnesses (including Peter and John) and other New Testament writers—appear throughout the Gospels.

WHY JESUS IS UNIQUE

When I (Josh) set out to challenge the Christian faith, I had to carefully consider whether Jesus really claimed to be God. And as we saw in chapter 5, the evidence led me to conclude that he did. But we can also take a different approach to the question of his identity. Rather than starting with a consideration of his unique claims as recorded in the Gospels, let's ask the question another way: *If God did step into history, what would we expect?* In other words, what impact would a divine person leave on the world? It turns out that Jesus fulfilled many of the things we might expect if God were to become human. Let's begin with the life and teachings of Jesus.

CHAPTER 9

WHAT IS UNIQUE ABOUT JESUS'S LIFE AND TEACHINGS?

History is full of belief systems and religious figures. Was Jesus unique from, say, Muhammad or the Buddha? In this chapter, we'll discuss whether Jesus is unlike any other human being who has walked the earth.

UNIQUE BIRTH

Jesus had a unique entrance into human history. The Gospels tell us that Jesus had no earthly father but was conceived of the Holy Spirit (Matt. 1:20, 22–23; Luke 1:35). No other historical religious figure was claimed to have been born of a virgin. (We'll discuss the historicity of the virgin conception in chapter 12).

While no historical religious figure has claimed to have had a virgin conception, some skeptics contend that Jesus's virgin birth was copied from the myths of pagan gods. However, many of the claims of certain gods being born of a virgin are outright false. Let's see what stories actually say about the birth of some of these pagan deities:

+ **Horus:** conceived when mother, Isis, had sex with Osiris's dead body
+ **Attis:** mother impregnated by eating the fruit of a tree that grew from Zeus's "seed"
+ **Krishna:** the eighth son born to his mother, Devaki
+ **Mithras:** born from a rock, not a virgin woman

These alleged virgin birth accounts of various pagan deities are simply unreal (as are many of the other alleged similarities with the life, death, and resurrection of Jesus, which we'll discuss in chapters 13 through 15). None of the origin stories for pagan deities describe actual historical events. Rather, they are mythical accounts divorced from history.

UNIQUE DEATH AND RESURRECTION

While many religious leaders and their followers have been martyred for their beliefs, Jesus is the only religious figure who is reported to have risen from the dead.

As with Jesus's virgin birth, it is easy to find online skeptics who also believe that Jesus's crucifixion and resurrection were copied from pagan dying and rising gods. Again, let's examine some of them here:

+ **Horus:** died by a snake bite; other accounts say he was poisoned but did not die
+ **Attis:** died by castrating himself or by being killed by a boar; no evidence of resurrection
+ **Adonis:** gored by a boar; no evidence of resurrection

+ **Krishna:** killed by a hunter; no evidence of resurrection
+ **Dionysus:** no evidence he was crucified; was reborn after being dismembered, eaten, and sewn into Zeus's thigh
+ **Osiris:** did not resurrect after death but lives on in the underworld[1]

The pagan gods died in substantially different ways than Jesus. And although the accounts of pagan rebirths are noted, none resemble the gospel accounts of Jesus's resurrection.

UNIQUE CLAIM TO BE GOD

Many religions have prophets and teachers who claimed to have special revelations from God. Islam, for instance, was founded by the prophet Muhammad. While there have been many other prophets within Christianity, it was founded by Jesus of Nazareth, who uniquely claimed to *be* God in the flesh. Jesus did not simply point the way to God, as other prophets do; he said he *is* the way (John 14:6).

UNIQUELY PREDICTED BY OLD TESTAMENT PROPHETS

Many other religious figures, such as Joseph Smith (the founder of the Church of Jesus Christ of Latter-day Saints), were viewed as prophets, or even allegedly had aspects of their lives prophesied by the prophets who preceded them. Yet the degree to which Jesus's birth, ministry, and death were foretold hundreds of years before his coming is unparalleled (see chapters 18 and 19).

UNIQUE SINLESS LIFE

The Bible tells us that Jesus is morally *perfect*. This is described in all four gospels, in reports of speeches by early Christian leaders in the book of Acts, in epistles written by four different authors, and in the book of Revelation (Matt. 4:1–11; 27:4, 19, 23–24; Mark 1:12–13, 24; Luke 4:1–13, 34; 23:14–15, 41, 47; John 5:19; 7:18; 8:46; Acts 3:14; 7:52; 22:14; 2 Cor. 5:21; Heb. 1:9; 4:15; 7:26; 1 Peter 1:19; 2:21–22; 3:18; 1 John 2:1– 2, 20; 3:5; Rev. 3:7). The consistent testimony of first-century Christians to the character of Jesus was that he was without sin, perfect in holiness and righteousness. There are no dissenting statements from Christians in the first century (or in the second century, for that matter). It seems to have been generally understood from the beginning of the Christian movement that its founder, Jesus Christ, was a morally and spiritually perfect human being.

Of course, religious adherents will think well of their leaders and possibly even exaggerate their moral greatness. What did Jesus think about himself? Just as Jesus never outrightly proclaimed, "I am God," neither did he explicitly claim to be sinless. But we can find instances of Jesus implicitly claiming to be without sin. For example, Jesus forgave other people's sins (Matt. 9:2–6; Mark 2:5–10; Luke 5:20–24; 7:47–49) and taught his followers to forgive others and to pray for God's forgiveness for their own sins (Matt. 6:12–15; 18:21–35; Mark 11:25; Luke 6:37; 11:4; 17:3–4). Yet Jesus never said anything about needing forgiveness himself, a surprising omission since good spiritual teachers typically use themselves as object lessons or at least model their teachings for their disciples.

The gospel of John records a hostile encounter between Jesus and the Pharisees in which the religious leaders questioned Jesus's authority and ability to testify on behalf of the Father. At one point, Jesus laid down the challenge, "Can any of you prove me guilty of sin?" (John 8:46 NIV). They couldn't. This shows that even Jesus's enemies knew he was a uniquely moral man, one of impeccable character. Also, Judas Iscariot, Herod Antipas, Pontius Pilate, Pilate's wife, the criminal crucified next to Jesus, and the centurion in charge at Jesus's crucifixion all declared that Jesus was innocent of any wrongdoing (Matt. 27:3–4, 19, 23–24; Luke 23:14–15, 40–41, 47).

But if Jesus was truly innocent, why was he executed? He was accused of committing blasphemy for considering himself the Son of God. However, if Jesus truly was the Son of God, it wasn't blasphemy but the truth. Jesus was an innocent man who was unjustly executed.

UNIQUE ROLE IN WORLD RELIGIONS

While Jesus is obviously the central figure of Christianity, did you know he is featured prominently in many other world religions as well? Here are just three of many:

+ **Hinduism:** Jesus is considered a wise teacher and a model for moral behavior.
+ **Buddhism:** Jesus is viewed as "enlightened" and a wise teacher.
+ **Islam:** Islam acknowledges many facts about Jesus, or "Isa," such as being born of a virgin and being a wise teacher, a prophet, and a miracle worker.

No other religious figure features as prominently in world religions as Jesus. This should tell us that there is something very special about him.

UNIQUE IMPACT ON HISTORY

No one has had a greater impact on human history than Jesus. In his book *Person of Interest*, J. Warner Wallace discusses the incredible ways the world seemed to be preparing for the coming of Jesus, as well as how Jesus forever altered the course of history.

Jesus arrived at a remarkable time for his message to be spread. Rome controlled much of the territory surrounding the Middle East, such as southern Europe, northern Africa, and the Mediterranean region. A common language and a great transportation system were in place so people could easily share the good news throughout their known world. Jesus also lived within the time of the Pax Romana, or Roman peace, in which Jews could peacefully and reasonably live in Roman cities and retain much of their custom and culture. There was also a greater degree of religious tolerance than ever before, so Jews could teach and worship. Accordingly, it seems that the scene was perfectly set for Jesus to arrive and his message to be spread.

Moreover, Wallace argues that Jesus had an unrivaled impact on the world apart from his religious teaching. No other person in history has been the subject of or inspiration for (explicitly or implicitly) more music, movies, and artwork across all styles and genres than Jesus. The growth of Christianity led to great innovations in architecture and technology (such as the printing press). Although many skeptics like Christopher Hitchens have accused religion of being the enemy of education and science, this is not the case for Christianity. Christians founded the earliest and most prominent universities and made some of the greatest scientific innovations and discoveries.

While it is true that all other religions inspire art and discovery, the impact that Jesus and Christianity have had on culture and history is unrivaled. To be clear, this doesn't prove that Jesus is God. But it fits with what we might expect if God were to enter history as a human being. These considerations should drive us to deeply consider the identity of such a remarkable figure.

CONCLUSION

Jesus is unique—unlike any other religious figure—in his birth, death and resurrection, claim to deity, fulfillment of prophecy, and sinless life. He is also featured prominently in many belief systems besides Christianity. No other person has had a greater impact on human history. What about Jesus's unique role as a miracle worker? Let's explore this next.

CHAPTER 10

WHAT IS UNIQUE ABOUT JESUS'S MIRACLES?

As we saw in chapter 8, Jesus was not just a good moral teacher. Given that he made the audacious claim of being divine, we only have so many conclusions we can draw about his identity. His divine claims are inseparable from his identity. Similarly, we cannot subtract the miracles of Jesus from his identity or ministry. The miracles of Jesus Christ are an essential part of his story and an essential part of the Christian faith. Removing the miracles from Christianity is not an option. As C. S. Lewis put it, "All the essentials of Hinduism would, I think, remain unimpaired if you subtracted the miraculous, and the same is almost true of Mohammedanism. But you cannot do that with Christianity. It is precisely the story of a great Miracle. A naturalistic Christianity leaves out all that is specifically Christian."[1]

The evidence that Jesus performed miraculous deeds is quite strong—so strong that New Testament scholar Craig Keener concluded, "There is a general consensus among scholars of early Christianity that Jesus was a miracle worker. . . . Most scholars today working on the subject thus accept the claim that Jesus was a healer and exorcist."[2]

MODERN SKEPTICAL SCHOLARS GENERALLY CONCEDE JESUS'S MIRACLES

In the nineteenth and twentieth centuries, many historians, philosophers, and even theologians were skeptical of miracles in general and of Jesus's miracles in particular. And yet many still concede that Jesus did things that people in his day understood as miracles. For instance, even though they believed that most of the miracle accounts in the Bible were legendary, German New Testament scholars Rudolf Bultmann and Joachim Jeremias conceded that Jesus performed acts that people interpreted as miraculous.[3] Such skepticism has not entirely disappeared—atheists remain adamant that belief in miracles is irrational—but scholarly skepticism has become surprisingly muted in recent years.

The reason contemporary scholarship has swung in the direction of acknowledging that Jesus performed miracles is simple: *the evidence is significant*. As scholars have applied their critical methodologies to the gospels, even when they accept only what their own methods can prove, they have found there is no escaping that Jesus performed marvelous feats of healing.

FIRST-CENTURY JEWS CONCEDED JESUS'S MIRACLES

One of the reasons scholars acknowledge that Jesus performed works that appeared to be miracles is because Jews who did not accept Jesus as the Messiah conceded the point in his own day and for centuries afterward.

Jesus's Contemporary Critics

Ancient Jewish opponents of Jesus and of early Christianity didn't deny that Jesus had performed miracles; instead, when they offered any opinion about them, they characterized them as sorcery or as the work of the devil. We can see this in the gospels themselves, where the scribes are reported as offering this explanation: "The scribes who came down from Jerusalem were saying, 'He is possessed by Beelzebul,' and 'by the prince of demons he casts out the demons'" (Mark 3:22 ESV; see also Matt. 9:34; 10:25; 12:24; Luke 11:15).

It is highly unlikely that the gospel writers, or their Christian sources, would volunteer this way of explaining away Jesus's miracles. We may therefore consider it certain that first-century Jewish critics of Christianity claimed that Jesus performed miracles by the power of the devil.

Josephus

Toward the end of the first century, the Jewish historian Josephus described Jesus as "a worker of amazing deeds."[4] This statement comes amid a passage controversial for its clear reflection of a Christian perspective (and no one thinks Josephus was a Christian). But scholars are generally in agreement that Josephus wrote the description of Jesus as "a worker of amazing deeds." If this were a Christian alteration, one would expect the language to be stock Christian terminology for miracles. The three terms most used in the New Testament for miracles are *dunamis* ("deed of power," "mighty work"), *teras* ("wonder"), and *sēmeion* ("sign"). All three of these words occur together in Acts 2:22, where the apostle Peter says that God performed "mighty works and wonders and signs" (ESV) through Jesus. But Josephus didn't use those words.

THE EARLY CHURCH HAD NO MOTIVE TO INVENT THE IDEA THAT JESUS WAS A MIRACLE WORKER

The Gospels and their sources all spoke of Jesus as performing miracles. This might be dismissed as evidence if we had reason to suspect that the early church would have felt it necessary to invent the miracle stories to "sell" Jesus to the Jews as a prophet or Messiah, or to gentiles as a redeemer. As it turns out, we have good evidence that they had no such motive.

Stories of Miracle Workers Were Rare During the Time of Jesus

Most people in the ancient Mediterranean world seem to have believed in the possibility of miraculous events, but stories of such occurrences were surprisingly uncommon. The modern assumption that ancient people were superstitious folk who easily believed in miracles is a half-truth at best. While it is true that ancient people did explain natural phenomena (especially in the heavenly bodies and in the forces of nature) as in some way to be the activity of the gods, that doesn't mean they uncritically accepted claims about supposed miracle workers.

No Reliable Accounts Exist of Other Jewish Miracle Workers in the Time of Jesus

Miraculous or supernatural acts have been reported throughout history, but with rare exceptions these miracles appear to have been isolated incidents. In this sense, supernatural events likely did occur in the first century apart from the direct involvement of Jesus Christ. What made Jesus unique was his well-deserved reputation as a successful miracle worker.

For example, there were Jews during the same general period as Jesus who performed exorcisms; Jesus himself even mentioned them (Matt. 12:27; Luke 11:19). But none of these Jewish exorcists seem to have gained widespread recognition (or notoriety, depending on one's point of view) for their work as Jesus did. Jesus's work in casting out demons was so impressive that some Jewish exorcists even tried to cast out evil spirits using the name of Jesus, an attempt that did not end well (Acts 19:13–16). Although some Jews in the general time period of the New Testament did seek miracles of exorcism and healing, few (other than Jesus) attained enough success to be remembered by name.

The Jews Did Not Assume That a Prophet or the Messiah Would Perform Miracles

A skeptic might suppose that even if miracle workers were rare in the New Testament era, the early Christians might have invented stories of Jesus performing miracles to buttress their claim that he was a prophet or the Messiah. In response, scholars have noted that Jews in that period did not assume that such figures would perform miracles.[5]

JESUS'S MIRACLES REVEALED HIM TO BE MORE THAN A TEACHER OR PROPHET

Everyone in the ancient world familiar with Jesus regarded him as a miracle worker. We have seen that Jesus's critics among his own Jewish people during his lifetime and afterward conceded his miracles but denied that God was their source. All of Jesus's followers agreed Jesus performed miracles by the power of God.

That Jesus performed a variety of miracles, especially exorcisms and healings, means that many popular modern theories about Jesus are out of touch with the historical reality attested by the evidence described previously. Notions of Jesus as merely a teacher of morals or a critic of the establishment are exposed as obvious attempts to modernize Jesus.

To understand the uniqueness of who Jesus is, we need to understand the significance of his miracles. Jesus never performed miracles to show off; he did not seek to gain anything for himself. His miracles were intimately bound up with his message that the kingdom of God was at hand and that it had arrived in his own person. When he began his ministry, his message was summed up by the announcement of the kingdom: "The time is fulfilled, and the kingdom of God is at hand. Repent, and believe in the gospel" (Mark 1:15).

This "gospel" or good news was the message that God was exercising his kingly rule in the fallen, sinful world in a new way. Miracles were an essential part of this message: "And he went throughout all Galilee, teaching in their synagogues and proclaiming the gospel of the kingdom and healing every disease and every affliction among the people" (Matt. 4:23 ESV; see also 9:35).

The best explanation for the unique way Jesus performed miracles is that he understood them to be expressions of the power of God in him (Luke 5:17). Jesus's miracles revealed the kingdom of God because Jesus *was* the King himself.

CHAPTER 11

IS JESUS REALLY THE ONLY WAY?

"How can you say Jesus is the only way? That's so closed-minded." This is a question, and a concern, we hear regularly from Christians and non-Christians. Given that smartphones have made the world much smaller and more interconnected, and we are more exposed to people of all sorts of beliefs and backgrounds, it's an understandable question! So far, we have examined ways in which Jesus is unique among other religious and historical figures. This chapter will explore what may be the most important way that Jesus is unique: *He is the one and only way to God.* Before we consider the seeming exclusiveness of such an idea, let's see if Jesus made such a claim in the first place.

JESUS

The clearest example of Jesus claiming to be the only way to God is in John 14:6: "I am the way, the truth, and the life. No one comes to the Father except through Me." Jesus did not say he is one of many ways, that he is delivering the truth, or that he can teach people the way to life. No, Jesus said he *is* the way, he *is* the truth, and he *is* the life.

Several chapters earlier in John's gospel, Jesus was challenged by a group of Jewish leaders who denied that he was the Messiah. Jesus told them, "If you do not believe that I am He, you will die in your sins" (John 8:24). Luke 10:16 records Jesus telling his followers something similar: "Whoever rejects me rejects him who sent me" (NIV).

In John 14, Jesus uses pastoral imagery to help the disciples understand his mission. The sheep are a symbol for God's people, and the sheep pen is a symbol for the kingdom of God. Jesus states that he is the shepherd who guides, protects, and lays down his life for the sheep. But he also says he is the gate by which the sheep may enter the pen. Just as no one can come to the Father except through Jesus (John 14:6), no one can enter the "sheep pen" except through the "gate," which is Jesus. He concludes with the audacious statement, "I and My Father are one" (John 10:30), another implicit claim that he is the only way to the Father.

In Matthew, Jesus uses gate imagery to describe the exclusive nature of Christianity. He said the "road that leads to destruction" is wide, while the gate is small and the "road that leads to life" is narrow "and only a few find it" (Matt. 7:13–14 NIV). Several chapters later Jesus says that the Father has given him authority because of their unique relationship: "No one knows the Son except the Father, and no one knows the Father except the Son and anyone to whom the Son chooses to reveal him" (Matt. 11:27 ESV).

JESUS'S FOLLOWERS

Jesus's followers also taught that Jesus is the only way to salvation. When Peter and John were brought before the

Sanhedrin, Peter boldly proclaimed the gospel of Jesus Christ, that "salvation is found in no one else, for there is no other name under heaven given to mankind by which we must be saved" (Acts 4:12 NIV). It doesn't get much clearer than that.

Paul and Silas had been jailed for preaching the gospel, and God sent a powerful earthquake to loosen all the prisoners' chains and open the prison doors. When the jailer realized what had happened and that none of the prisoners had tried to escape, he asked Paul and Silas what he must do to be saved. They replied, "Believe in the Lord Jesus" (Acts 16:31 NIV).

Paul also tells us in 1 Timothy 2:5 that "there is one God and one mediator between God and mankind, the man Christ Jesus" (NIV), reiterating that Jesus is the only way to God.

Following the teachings of Jesus, the apostles and New Testament writers brought the message to the world that Jesus was the only way to God.

OBJECTION: THAT'S NOT FAIR!

The obvious objection to Jesus being the only way to salvation is that it isn't fair. What about people who sincerely believe in their religion? What about people in remote locations throughout history who never had the opportunity to hear the gospel? Given this legitimate concern, how should we respond to objections like these?

God Is Evident in Creation

We have God's moral code written on our hearts, and creation itself is a testament to a creator. Romans 1:18–20 tells us that God has made himself known through his creation, and so "people are without excuse" (NIV) for their wrong behavior. Romans 2:14–15 teaches that everyone has a general sense of right and wrong because it is "written on their hearts" (NIV). Psalm 19:1 says, "The heavens declare the glory of God; the skies proclaim the work of his hands" (NIV). The Bible makes clear that everyone has sufficient evidence to know that God exists.

In Acts 17 Paul pointed out the innate religiousness of the Athenian people, who had an altar to "AN UNKNOWN GOD" so as not to offend any gods they were unaware of. He then proclaimed to the people that the one they were looking for is the Christian God, who proved his sovereignty over creation by raising Jesus from the dead. This scene displays how all people have an innate knowledge of something "out there" beyond us, a desire to worship.

Acts 17 teaches us that many people have a general spiritual awareness or a belief in a general creator God. But what about those who don't have an apostle Paul in their lives to tell them about their "unknown god"? What hope do they have for salvation?

Seek and You Will Find

Jesus promises that those who seek him will find him. He says, "Ask and it will be given to you; seek and you will find; knock and the door will be opened to you. For everyone who asks receives; the one who seeks finds; and to the one who knocks, the door will be opened" (Matt. 7:7–8 NIV). No one can say that they genuinely sought God and God did not reveal himself.

God has also placed people in certain times and places so that they *would* seek him. Let's return to Paul's speech to the Athenians. He told them, "From one man he made all the nations, that they should inhabit the whole earth; and he marked out their appointed times in history and the boundaries of their lands. God did this so that they would seek him and perhaps reach out for him and find him, though he is not far from any one of us" (Acts 17:26–27 NIV). Some people argue that God is unfair since there are people out of the reach of the gospel who will be lost because they never heard about Jesus. These verses turn that argument on its head. God purposely determined the place and time that people would be born *so that they would seek him.*

This leads to our next point.

Christianity Is Inclusive

Christianity may be exclusive in that Jesus is the only way to salvation, but Christianity is also inclusive, because salvation is available to anyone. In the Old Testament, God accepted "outsiders" like Ruth, Melchizedek, and Rahab. We learn in the New Testament that God "wants all people to be saved and to come to a knowledge of the truth" (1 Tim. 2:4 NIV) and that God wants "everyone to come to repentance" (2 Peter 3:9 NIV). And in what may be the most famous verse in the entire Bible, Jesus tells us that whoever believes in him will be granted eternal life (John 3:16).

In the Great Commission, Jesus commanded his disciples to "go and make disciples of all nations" (Matt. 28:19 NIV). On the day of Pentecost, the believers spoke in various languages, which was a sign of all the peoples to whom the gospel would be spread (Acts 2:1–12). Revelation 5:9 tells us that Jesus's blood "purchased for God persons from every tribe and language and people and nation" (NIV). Over the centuries, countless missionaries have made it their life's work to share the gospel in every region of the world, no matter how dangerous. Many of them have done so at the cost of their lives.

What about You?

Is it okay if we make this personal? If you are reading this book, you have learned about Jesus of Nazareth. You learned in this chapter that Jesus is the only way to salvation. Perhaps you believe it is unfair that other people may not have had the opportunity to hear about Jesus. But *you* have. If you are a Christian, this should inspire you to go out and reach the unevangelized. If you aren't a Christian, you have sufficient evidence to decide about Christ, and you cannot say you never had the opportunity to hear and to respond to the gospel.

CONCLUSION

Nowadays, it is intolerant to claim that one religion is the only right way. Yet this is what Jesus and his earliest followers claimed: Jesus is the only way to salvation. While people may call this claim intolerant, what matters is whether it is *true*. If Jesus claimed to be God, if he stands apart as a unique person in history, and if he was able to perform great wonders to confirm that he is indeed God in the flesh, then we must accept his teachings and commands as well. Jesus is the only way to God because he *is* God.

CHAPTER 12

WAS JESUS REALLY BORN OF A VIRGIN?

A FEW YEARS AGO, I (SEAN) HAD A CONVERSATION WITH AN atheist friend on a range of faith issues. One of the topics we discussed was the virgin birth. Before we even talked about the evidence that Jesus might have been born of a virgin, he asserted that a virgin birth is biologically impossible, and thus such a claim is not scientifically credible. He was certainly right that a virgin birth is not biologically possible. But does that mean the story is false? No. If the virgin birth were biologically possible, then it wouldn't be a miracle. Even in the first century, people knew that virgins didn't give birth. That was exactly why God chose to enter history in this manner—as a divine sign. For miracles to work as authenticating signs, which is how they function in the Bible, they must stand out from the normal course of nature. That miracles deviate from the normal course of nature cannot be taken as evidence against their occurrence because this is precisely what miracles are meant to do!

If God exists, then miracles are possible. If God does *not* exist, then miracles are *not* possible. And if God created the universe, including all life on earth and the laws of nature, then it's no problem for him to miraculously intervene in the normal course of events and enter human history through a virgin birth.

Of course, we have to examine the evidence that Jesus was born of a virgin. Yet we must make an important point: *your acceptance of the virgin birth depends largely on your worldview.* If you believe that God does not exist and that everything has a natural explanation, then a virgin birth must be ruled out prior to considering the facts. But if you believe in the existence of God, or are minimally open to it, then you might be persuaded to believe that Jesus was born of a virgin. While the virgin birth cannot be proven, since there were no eyewitnesses to confirm how Mary was impregnated, there are several good reasons to believe it truly happened.

THE IDEA OF THE VIRGIN BIRTH ORIGINATED VERY EARLY

One way to dismiss the story of the virgin birth is to claim that it must have arisen as a legend or myth. However, there are reasons to believe the story arose very early within Christianity.

Matthew and Luke Were Written Within the Lifetimes of Eyewitnesses

The New Testament contains two accounts of the miraculous conception of Jesus by the Holy Spirit, found in the opening chapters of the gospels of Matthew and Luke. Despite the debates over the dating of Matthew and Luke, the majority view is that these books were written sometime between AD 70 and 95, within the century that Jesus was born and less than sixty years after his death (in AD 30 or 33). That does not allow much time for a legend or myth to arise and take such detailed forms as we find in Matthew and Luke.

A good case can be made that at least one of these gospels was written much earlier than the majority view. The gospel of Luke is the first of a two-volume work on the origins of Christianity. The gospel, which is part one, focuses on Jesus from his conception and birth through his death, resurrection, and ascension. The book of Acts, part two, is an account of the first thirty years or so of the Christian church, from the ascension of Jesus to Paul's house arrest in Rome (ca. 60–62). This means that AD 62 is the earliest Acts could have been completed, but it also at least suggests that it was finished not long after that date, likely sometime in the 60s.

If Acts was written in the 60s, then the gospel of Luke, which was likely written earlier than Acts, was probably written no later than the 60s. This would mean that Luke's account of Jesus's conception and birth was written no more than about thirty years after Jesus's death. In any case, as noted earlier, most scholars accept that Matthew and Luke were written in the first century. Whether we date these gospels to the 60s or later, viewing such writings about Jesus as mythology, considering how close in time they were to their subject, is probably wrong.

Matthew and Luke Give Independent Testimonies to the Virgin Birth

Comparing Matthew and Luke's accounts of Jesus's conception and birth demonstrates that neither gospel writer invented the story—that is, the basic storyline was already in place sometime before either gospel was written. This is the case because

their two accounts differ so greatly and yet share many striking similarities. It is the combination of these similarities and
differences that is important.

First, consider the differences. Matthew begins with a
genealogy tracing Jesus's ancestry from Abraham to Joseph.
He then narrates the story of Joseph being told by an angel in
a dream to take Mary as his wife. Matthew reports that Mary
gave birth to a son in Bethlehem and then was visited by magi
who had seen his star in the east. After the magi left, Joseph
took Mary and Jesus to Egypt to escape Herod's slaughter,
returning to Nazareth after Herod's death.

Luke's account, for starters, is more than twice as long
as Matthew's. It begins with an angel's announcement to
Zechariah that his barren, elderly wife Elizabeth will have
a child, followed by that angel's announcement to the young
virgin Mary that she will have a child despite not having con-
summated her marriage. Luke then narrates Mary's visit to
Elizabeth to see John's birth. Next, Luke tells about Joseph
taking Mary to Bethlehem, where she gives birth to Jesus, and
about the shepherds coming to see the child. They then go
to Jerusalem, where Jesus is circumcised and where a prophet
named Simeon and a prophetess named Anna recognize the
child as the Messiah. The family goes home to Nazareth but
returns to Jerusalem every Passover; when Jesus is twelve, he
stays behind when his parents leave, talking to the teachers
in the temple. After Luke's account of John's baptism of Jesus
when they are both adults, Luke gives a very different genealogy, tracing Jesus's ancestry backward from Joseph to Adam.

The two narratives don't have a single passage or unit
of material in common. The differences are especially note-

worthy because elsewhere the gospels of Matthew and Luke do have a considerable amount of material in common. Thus, the complete lack of parallel material in the infancy narratives makes it all but certain that neither gospel writer drew on the other's narrative.

Despite the fact that Matthew and Luke read so differently, there are similarities. Consider a long list of these similarities:

+ Mary was Jesus's mother (Matt. 1:16, 18; 2:11; Luke 2:5–7, 16, 34).
+ Joseph and Mary were betrothed but not married when Mary became pregnant (Matt. 1:18; Luke 1:27–38; 2:5).
+ Mary was a virgin when she conceived Jesus (Matt. 1:23–25; Luke 1:27, 34).
+ An angel announced the birth of the child (Matt. 1:20, 24; Luke 1:26, 30, 34–38; 2:9–13).
+ An angel explained that the child was conceived by the Holy Spirit (Matt. 1:20; Luke 1:35).
+ An angel stated that the child was to be named Jesus (Matt. 1:21; Luke 1:31).
+ An angel declared that Jesus would save his people (Matt. 1:21) or be their Savior (Luke 2:11).
+ Jesus was descended from David (Matt. 1:1, 17; Luke 1:32, 69; 3:31; see also Mark 10:47–48).
+ Joseph was a descendant of David (Matt. 1:1–6, 20; Luke 2:4).
+ Jesus was to rule as the Davidic king of the Jews (Matt. 2:2; Luke 1:32–33).

+ Jesus was the Christ (Matt. 1:17; 2:4; Luke 2:11).
+ Jesus was born during the reign of Herod the Great (Matt. 2:1, 3, 7, 12–22; Luke 1:5).
+ Jesus was born in Bethlehem (Matt. 2:1; Luke 2:4–7).
+ Visitors went to see Jesus in Bethlehem (Matt. 2:11; Luke 2:15–16).
+ The birth of Jesus was the occasion of great "joy" for the visitors (Matt. 2:10; Luke 2:10).
+ Jesus was born after Joseph and Mary began living together (Matt. 1:25; Luke 2:5–7).
+ Joseph and Mary raised Jesus as their son (Matt. 1:16; 2:13–23; 13:55; Luke 2:16, 33, 48; see also Mark 6:3; John 1:45; 6:42).
+ Jesus grew up in Nazareth (Matt. 2:23; Luke 1:26; 2:39, 51; see also Mark 1:9, 24; John 1:45, 46).

The number and specificity of these similarities demonstrate that they go back to a common origin. Yet they cannot both originate from a common earlier story or narrative (written or oral) because if they did, they would have at least some narrative material in common. Consider this probable scenario: Matthew gives his account from the perspective of Joseph, and Luke gives his account from the perspective of Mary. This scenario suggests Matthew relied on Joseph's eyewitness account (even if he received this testimony through other family members such as James), and Luke relied on Mary's eyewitness account. This means that the two accounts derive from different sources that happened to include many of the same ideas, even if presented very differently.

CONCLUSION

We may not be able to prove with certainty that Jesus was born of a virgin. But if you accept the existence of God, or are at least open to the possibility, then we think a good case can be made, based on the evidence presented, that the virgin birth is the best explanation of the biblical data.

SECTION 3

CONCLUSION

We've seen all the ways that Jesus stands apart from every other person who has ever lived. He had a unique life and death and an unrivaled impact on human history. While supernatural acts are ascribed to other religious figures, the kinds of miracles Jesus performed and the reasons for which he performed them are unique. And Jesus is the sole figure of any major world religion who claimed to be God.

JESUS IS NOT A COPYCAT SAVIOR

As a young man growing up in a Christian home, I (Sean) had little reason to question the teachings of my parents. Christianity made sense, and I knew my parents loved me and wanted the best for me. But when I entered college, I encountered new and challenging people and ideas. One idea that caught me off guard was the idea that Christianity was borrowed from ancient pagan mystery religions. In other words, Christianity was nothing more than a patchwork of pagan and mystery religions stitched together to create a copycat religion.

This objection was one factor that spun me into a mild faith crisis. Now I can look back and see how unsophisticated this objection is, but at the time it was quite unsettling. And I was certainly not alone in wondering whether Christianity is true. This same idea and ideas like it have been popularized in movies such as *Zeitgeist*, *The Da Vinci Code*, and *Religulous*.

While it is tempting to write off these works as inconsequential, the ideas they peddle continue to have sweeping influence. The cover of Dan Brown's book claims it has sold more than eighty million copies. And copycat arguments appear frequently on the internet. We regularly receive questions about this objection from both students and adults. Although the "mythicist" position is almost entirely rejected in academic circles, it continues to have an influence on the wider public and warrants a response.

CHAPTER 13

WHAT ARE THE FEATURES OF MYSTERY RELIGIONS?

Jesus is sometimes dismissed as a mythical figure who is a blend of various pagan dying and rising gods. To respond to these allegations, we must first understand what these mystery religions were like.[1]

BACKGROUND

During the Roman Empire, the most influential religions other than Judaism and Christianity were the mystery religions. In broad terms, these religions of the Mediterranean region can be divided into two groups: (1) state or civil religions, which achieved a certain level of cult status, and (2) private, or individualistic, religions.

The cults most often compared with Christianity are the cults of Demeter and Dionysus from Greece, the cults of Cybele and Attis from the Phrygian region of Asia Minor, the cults of Isis and Osiris from Egypt, the cult of Adonis from Syria and Palestine, and the cult of Mithras from Persia (modern Iran). Many of these names may sound familiar, as we compared some of these alleged dying and rising gods with Jesus in chapter 9.

Because these religions were practiced during the formative years of Christianity, questions arose: Did early Christians copy or borrow certain rituals and key concepts from these pagan religions and weave them into Christianity to make it more appealing to potential converts? Did Christianity plagiarize these mystery religions? Are there any aspects genuinely unique to Christianity? Let's begin by examining the key features of these mystery religions.

Note that we have limited information about the mystery religions, partly because of a vow of secrecy imposed on the initiates. That's why they're called *mystery religions*. Their beliefs and practices also varied from place to place and from time to time. What follows is an overview of what is known about those mythologies. We highlight three key features of the mystery religions here, and then we will contrast them with Christianity in the next chapter, demonstrating enormous worldview differences between the two.

CYCLICAL VIEW OF LIFE

Adherents of the mystery religions found deep meaning in the annual vegetation cycle, in which crops would die in the fall and then come back to life in the spring. This cycle of plant life inspired the belief of a similar cycle in humans, giving rise to the hope of a life after death.

This cycle is also symbolized through mystery religions' central myths about their deities rising to life after death, often acted out in dramatic form for cult members. The mystery deities were tightly bound up in and correlated to the annual vegetation cycle, so this was a repetitive, yearly process. This is why many of the gods of growth are also gods of death. But it's important to note that the deities' death and rebirth was always viewed as a *metaphor* for the life cycles of vegetation and humans.

SECRET CEREMONIES

Secret ceremonies were important to mystery religions. Most often they were initiation rites that would unite initiates while separating them from others. In some cults, redemption was not earned through learning specific teachings but simply by gaining a type of higher knowledge through the cult's secret ceremonies.

LITTLE TO NO EMPHASIS ON DOCTRINE

Mystery religions did not place a high premium on intellect, truth, or doctrinal soundness. They were less concerned about having correct teaching (orthodoxy) and intellectual rigor than about feeding and exciting the emotions of their initiates and followers. Once followers achieved union with their god through trumped-up emotions, two other goals became the focus of the mystery religions: salvation (or redemption) and immortality. This was secured through initiation rites and purification ceremonies.

The salvation offered in these religions makes clear their appeal to people who were otherwise helpless before an implacable fate and the erratic will of often capricious gods. But the fact that people recognized their need for salvation and immortality highlights some important truths: the tragic flaw of sin and the need for the conclusive work of a redeemer.

Proponents of the claim that Christianity borrowed from these mystery religions will state that cultists, upon gaining union with their deity, would be resurrected with their deity and thus gain immortality. Certainly, the use of such language would lead one to agree that it sounds as if mystery cults influenced Christianity.

SUMMARY

Mystery religions are secretive by nature, and so there is much we don't know about them. But we do know they were heavily influenced by the annual vegetation cycle of the "death" and "rebirth" of crops. The deities of the cults personified this dying and rising motif, which some argue inspired the story of the death and resurrection of Jesus. But as noted, it is important to remember that mystery religion deities were always viewed as *metaphors* for the vegetation cycle.

DYING AND RISING GODS

Now that we have discussed the general similarities between the mystery religions, let's look at the most common myths and deities that are claimed to have influenced Christianity, specifically the account of Jesus's resurrection.

Isis and Osiris

Osiris is an ancient Egyptian god who was introduced to the Greeks around 300 BC as an adaption of the Greek god

Dionysus. The myth of Osiris is that his brother killed him and chopped him into fourteen pieces. His wife, Isis, found all but one of the pieces and reassembled Osiris. It is uncertain whether Osiris was raised back to life or continued to live in the underworld. In either case, this would not be considered a resurrection in the same manner of Jesus's resurrection.

Cybele and Attis

The goddess Cybele loved a shepherd named Attis, but when he was unfaithful to her, she drove him insane. In his insanity, Attis castrated himself and bled to death. Cybele's grief brought death to the world, but when she returned Attis to life, the world came back to life as well. Here, we see an obvious connection between the deaths of Attis and the world, as well as Attis and the world both being brought back to life. The myth of Attis has a direct link to the vegetation cycle. In fact, worshipers of Cybele and Attis enacted this myth to grant them a good crop.

Adonis

There are two versions of the myth of Adonis. In one, he is loved by the goddesses Aphrodite and Persephone, and Zeus decides Adonis will live with each goddess for half of the year. In the second myth, Adonis is killed by a boar and mourned by Aphrodite. It is only in later versions of the myth, which appear after the rise of Christianity, that Adonis is brought back to life. Thus, it seems that Christianity influenced the myth of Adonis, not the other way around. Also, there is no evidence that Adonis was ever worshiped as a dying and rising god.

Summary

From these three examples, we should be able to see that there is little resemblance between alleged dying and rising gods and Jesus of Nazareth. None of the myths present anything close to Jesus's resurrection. And when cultists reenacted the death and rising of their god, it was always understood to be a metaphor of the changing of the seasons.

CONCLUSION

The purpose of this chapter was to gain a better understanding of pagan mystery religions, which are alleged to have influenced the creation of Christianity. The secretive nature of these cults makes it difficult to gain insight into their beliefs and practices, but some key features, such as an emphasis on the yearly vegetation cycle, the importance of secret ceremonies, and a lack of specific doctrine, have shown that these mystery religions have little to no similarity to Christianity.

In the next chapter, we will directly address what differentiates Christianity from these pagan mystery religions.

CHAPTER 14

HOW DOES CHRISTIANITY DIFFER FROM THE MYSTERY RELIGIONS?

THE CLAIM THAT CHRISTIANITY WAS COPIED FROM ANCIENT pagan mystery religions seemed plausible at first because I (Sean) saw many apparent similarities. But as I probed deeper, I realized that many of these similarities were merely on the surface. Those who defend this view often overplay the similarities and downplay the differences. In this chapter, we'll show how Christianity is fundamentally different from these pagan mystery religions in a range of vital areas. Let's start with the historical nature of the Christian faith.

HISTORICALLY BASED

The mystery religions centered on the natural vegetative cycle, and thus many of the pagan dying and rising gods served as metaphors for this cycle. None of them are genuine historical figures, and adherents to mystery religions knew that. In contrast, the Bible depicts Jesus as a real historical person. The gospel accounts contain many passages full of evidential treasures for anyone to examine, especially those who wonder about the truth of Christianity.

It is central to Christianity that God himself entered into human history, lived with us, died publicly on a Roman cross, rose again, and appeared to many people. Consider a few passages that indicate the historical nature of the biblical account:

> Now in the fifteenth year of the reign of Tiberius Caesar, Pontius Pilate being governor of Judea, Herod being tetrarch of Galilee, his brother Philip tetrarch of Iturea and the region of Trachonitis, and Lysanias tetrarch of Abilene, while Annas and Caiaphas were high priests, the word of God came to John the son of Zacharias in the wilderness. And he went into all the region around the Jordan, preaching a baptism of repentance for the remission of sins. (Luke 3:1–3)

> If Christ is not risen, then our preaching is empty and your faith is also empty. Yes, and we are found false witnesses of God, because we have testified of God that He raised up Christ, whom He did not raise up—if in fact the dead do not rise. For if the dead do not rise, then Christ is not risen. And if Christ is not risen, your faith is futile; you are still in your sins! (1 Cor. 15:14–17)

Note the amount of historical detail that Luke provided in just three verses: real-life names, dates, and geographical locations. These are the hallmarks of true history, not mythology. Luke wanted his readers to know that he carefully researched his gospel. Likewise, Paul wanted his readers to know that Jesus's resurrection was a historical fact. If it weren't, then our faith would be meaningless and we'd be hopelessly lost in our sins. Thus, the biblical writers made it perfectly clear that Jesus was a real person who lived in history and had many witnesses to the events of his life. Unlike the pagan deities of mystery religions, Jesus is an actual historical figure.

PUBLIC PROCLAMATION

Mystery religions were just that—*mysteries*. The teachings and rituals were secret, reserved only for initiates. This is a stark contrast with Christianity. While the early Christians were known for certain "insider" rituals like baptism, the Eucharist, and prayers, these were not practiced solely in secret but were performed and proclaimed in public. Even today, many churches may reserve practices such as baptism and the Lord's Supper for committed Christians or church members while still allowing visitors to view the practices. The public proclamation of Christianity is made clear in several passages of Scripture.

> Men of Israel, hear these words: Jesus of Nazareth, a man attested to you by God with mighty works and wonders and signs that God did through him in your midst, as you yourselves know—this Jesus, delivered up according to the definite plan and foreknowledge of God, you crucified and killed by the hands of lawless men. God raised him up, loosing the pangs of death, because it was not possible for him to be held by it. (Acts 2:22–24 ESV)

> Everyone who acknowledges me before men, I also will acknowledge before my Father who is in heaven, but whoever denies me before men, I also will deny before my Father who is in heaven. (Matt. 10:32–33 ESV)

> We did not follow cunningly devised fables when we made known to you the power and coming of our Lord Jesus Christ, but were eyewitnesses of His majesty. (2 Peter 1:16)

Christianity was a very public religion, and its being a public religion often got its adherents into serious trouble. For instance, the apostles were threatened, beaten, and put in prison for *publicly* proclaiming the gospel (Acts 4:1–3; 5:17–42). Unlike the secretive nature of pagan religions, Christianity has always been a public religion, open for all to scrutinize.

DOCTRINE MATTERS

Mystery religions emphasized emotional experiences rather than doctrine. In contrast, the Christian Scriptures place a high importance on teaching and believing. These are examples from both the Old and New Testaments:

> Therefore you shall lay up these words of mine in your heart and in your soul, and bind them as a sign on your hand, and they shall be as frontlets between your eyes. You shall teach them to your children, speaking of them when you sit in your house, when you walk by the way, when you lie down, and when you rise up. And you shall write them

on the doorposts of your house and on your gates, that your days and the days of your children may be multiplied in the land of which the LORD swore to your fathers to give them, like the days of the heavens above the earth.

For if you carefully keep all these commandments which I command you to do—to love the LORD your God, to walk in all His ways, and to hold fast to Him—then the LORD will drive out all these nations from before you, and you will dispossess greater and mightier nations than yourselves. (Deut. 11:18–23)

Jesus came and spoke to them, saying, "All authority has been given to Me in heaven and on earth. Go therefore and make disciples of all the nations, baptizing them in the name of the Father and of the Son and of the Holy Spirit, teaching them to observe all things that I have commanded you; and lo, I am with you always, even to the end of the age." (Matt. 28:18–20)

He must hold firm to the trustworthy word as taught, so that he may be able to give instruction in sound doctrine and also to rebuke those who contradict it. (Titus 1:9 ESV)

These few verses illustrate just how important truth and sound doctrine are to Christianity. Over the centuries, Christian leaders have assembled creeds and confessions to codify the core beliefs of Christianity. Furthermore, the Bible is accessible, whether physical versions, sold in every bookstore, or online versions. The teachings of Christianity are publicly available.

CONCLUSION

If Christianity has similarities to mystery religions, it is only because *all* religions have similarities. They have holy books, places of worship, ceremonies, and dogma. They may teach about salvation, redemption, proper living, and life after death. So it is no surprise that Christianity has some things in common with mystery religions.

But when we dig beneath these surface similarities, we see that Christianity is significantly different from mystery religions. Christianity is firmly centered in history, while mystery religions are rooted in myth. The gospel is not a secret. The gospel has always been preached publicly for all to hear. Christianity is not a mere emotional experience but emphasizes true belief through sound doctrine and righteous living. Bottom line: Christianity is fundamentally different from mystery religions.

Let's conclude our comparison of Christianity and mystery religions by examining five reasons why we should reject the belief that these religions influenced Christianity.

CHAPTER 15

CAN WE REJECT THE COPYCAT THEORY?

The previous two chapters sufficiently undermine the claim that Christianity borrowed core ideas from ancient mystery religions. Christianity and the mystery religions have insurmountable differences. Yet, to put it to rest, let's consider five specific reasons why we should reject the copycat theory as a sufficient explanation for the origin of Christianity.

REASON #1: TRUE TO ITS JEWISH ROOTS, CHRISTIANITY DID NOT ACCEPT OTHER GODS

Unlike the gentiles of the early Christian era, Jews refused to blend their religion with other religions, which was the sin of syncretism. Mystery religions were *inclusive*, but Judaism and Christianity were *exclusive*. Generally, Jews intensely resisted pagan ideas.

Furthermore, Paul had been trained as an orthodox Jew. He held steadfastly to orthodox beliefs about the one true God and would have been unwilling to compromise them for pagan mythology, no matter the cost. Let's look at the biblical data:

Circumcised on the eighth day, of the people of Israel, of
the tribe of Benjamin, a Hebrew of Hebrews; as to the law,
a Pharisee; as to zeal, a persecutor of the church; as to righteousness under the law, blameless. But whatever gain I had,
I counted as loss for the sake of Christ. (Phil. 3:5–7 ESV)

I was advancing in Judaism beyond many of my own age
among my people, so extremely zealous was I for the traditions of my fathers. (Gal. 1:14 ESV)

In these passages and in his defense when on trial, Paul
describes his strict training by the Pharisees. But he explains
that he was transformed only when and because he realized
that the risen Christ was indeed the promised Messiah (Phil.
3:8–10; Gal. 1:15, 22–23; Acts 24:14–15; 26:5–23). Neither
Paul nor any of the other early leaders of Christianity would
have adopted the beliefs and practices of pagan religions and
then expected their fellow Jews to follow them. That would
have been unheard of.

REASON #2: THE DIFFERENCES BETWEEN CHRISTIANITY AND MYSTERY RELIGIONS OUTWEIGH THE SIMILARITIES

Christianity and mystery religions may use parallel *terms*, but
they do not have parallel *concepts*. For example, Christianity
and mystery religions (as well as many other religions throughout history) teach about salvation. But what Christianity
means by salvation and what mystery religions mean by salvation have little in common.

The same goes for the concept of resurrection. Osiris

is often considered a dying and rising god. But the earliest accounts have him leading a life beyond the tomb that nearly replicates earthly life. He rules over the land of the dead and will never again be among the living. And perhaps most significantly, Egyptians did not believe in bodily resurrection. Pagan notions of "resurrection" are completely different from the Christian concept of Christ's (and our) resurrection.

REASON #3: PARALLELS BETWEEN THE TWO PROVE NOTHING

Have you ever heard about the massive British ship carrying thousands of people that struck an iceberg in April and sank on its maiden voyage in the North Atlantic? You may recognize this as the true story of the sinking of the *Titanic*. But you're wrong. We're talking about the *Titan*, the fictional ship from Morgan Robertson's 1898 book, *The Wreck of the Titan; or, Futility*, written fourteen years before the sinking of the *Titanic*. It's obvious that the story of the *Titanic* is simply a rip-off of Robertson's fictional story, right? Wrong. While the sinking of the *Titanic* certainly has uncanny resemblances to the story about the *Titan*, this does not mean the *Titanic* never existed. The similarity to the story about the *Titan* is strange, yet we have news reports and eyewitness testimony from survivors to confirm that the sinking of the *Titanic* is a true historical event.

Similarly, fictional accounts of dying and rising gods would not undermine the historical reality of the life, death, and resurrection of Jesus. The presence of parallels alone proves nothing about Christianity allegedly borrowing from mystery religions or about the historicity of Jesus, which we have already discussed in previous chapters. If you want to show that one religion influenced the other, you must prove there is a causal connection between the two. This leads into our next point.

REASON #4: CHRISTIANITY SEEMS TO HAVE INFLUENCED MYSTERY RELIGIONS, NOT THE OTHER WAY AROUND

Virtually all the evidence of ancient Greco-Roman mystery religions comes from the second to fourth centuries. So how can we explain away first-century Christianity by comparing it to religions that arose decades or centuries later? Sure, it's possible there were first-century precursors to the mystery cults of the second century and beyond, but this is an argument from silence. There is no evidence that Christianity was influenced by or modeled after contemporary mystery religions.

For example, there is a mystery religion ritual called the "taurobolium," in which initiates were bathed in the blood of a dying bull. This has been alleged to be a source for Christian teachings about being sprinkled by Jesus's blood (1 Peter 1:2) or being washed in the blood of the Lamb (Rev. 7:14). Could this pagan ritual have influenced the biblical writers? The core problem is the dating of the ritual, which first appeared in the West in the second century, *after* the emergence of Christian teaching. Thus, the blood bath ritual may have been changed because of Christian influence. Regardless, it's clear that New Testament teaching about the shedding of blood should not be linked to a pagan source but instead to the Passover and the temple sacrifices of the Old Testament.

Bottom line: If there is any connection between Christianity and mystery religions, it is that Christianity influenced mystery religions, not the other way around.

REASON #5: THE DEATH OF JESUS IS UNIQUE

The death of Jesus is strikingly different from the deaths of various gods of the mystery religions for at least six reasons:

1. Jesus's Death Was Sacrificial

According to Christianity, Jesus's death was sacrificial. His death substituted his righteousness for the sins of each individual who has put his or her faith in Jesus. He takes on their sin and shields them from punishment so that they will not have to bear it (see John 10:11; 15:13; 1 John 3:16). The deaths of pagan gods were not sacrificial.

2. Jesus Died for the Sins of Everyone

Jesus did far more than die on behalf of his friends. He died for the sins of his immediate friends and followers and all those who would believe in him in the future (see Rom. 3:23–26; 1 Cor. 15:3; 2 Cor. 5:14–15, 17–19, 21; Gal. 1:3–4). It has never been claimed that any of the pagan deities died to save people from their sin.

3. Jesus Died Only Once

The deaths of the mystery religion gods were cyclical in nature, but Jesus is never represented in Scripture as dying and rising over and over again. This would lead to a hopeless despair that there is no escaping the repetition of the yearly cycle, in which vegetation dies, kings decline and die, and people live toward death. Instead, the biblical pattern is that Jesus died once for all and came to give abundant life (see Heb. 7:27; 9:25–28; 10:10–14; John 10:10).

4. Jesus's Death Was a Historical Event

Unlike the pagan gods who would "die and rise" cyclically with the annual seasons, Jesus was a historical figure who died once and then rose again on the third day. The death of Jesus is not a mythical claim but a historical fact rooted in history (see Acts 2:22–23; 1 Cor. 15:14, 17).

5. Jesus's Death Was Voluntary

Jesus made it plain that he would lay down his life at a time of his own choosing (John 12:20–33). Although the gospel accounts tell us that the religious leaders attempted to arrest Jesus and kill him, Jesus always slipped away from them and thwarted their plans because it was not yet the right time (see John 7:30; 10:17–18; 19:10–11). But when he knew the time had come, he quietly submitted to arrest in the garden of Gethsemane (John 13:1).

6. Jesus's Death Ended in Victory, Not Defeat

The historical record regarding Jesus does not end on a bloody cross or in a rock-cut tomb. It ends with an empty tomb and an ascension. The resurrection provides hope and the promise of eternal life. The end is triumph, not tragedy (see 1 Cor. 15:54–55).

CONCLUSION

As you can see, there is no evidence that mystery religions had any influence on Christianity. If anything, Christianity influenced mystery religions, not the other way around. The meaning and purpose of Jesus's death and resurrection are worlds apart from the cyclical view of time held by the mystery religions.

CHAPTER 16

DOES ARCHAEOLOGY CONFIRM THE EXISTENCE OF JESUS?

Unlike the ancient mystery religions, Christianity is historically based. Thus, we would expect to find corroboration in the historical and archaeological record for the people, places, and events described in the Gospels. Over the past 150 years, archaeology has contributed to a deeper understanding of the cultural context of Jesus *and* provided corroboration for the events and people recorded in the Gospels. While new discoveries are ongoing, here are some key archaeological finds that help confirm the gospel accounts about Jesus. We have visited many of these places and seen these discoveries with our own eyes.

PEOPLE

Aside from Jesus and his disciples, the Gospels are full of other people, some important to the recorded accounts and some simply mentioned in passing. It is critical to understand that these people are not mythical figures but real, historical people recorded by Matthew, Mark, Luke, and John. While we should not expect to find archaeological evidence for every person named in the Gospels—as they lived nearly two thousand years ago—every bit of evidential corroboration we find for a name listed in the Gospels lends credibility to the fact that Jesus of Nazareth is a true historical figure as well.

Lysanias

In Luke 3:1, Luke mentions that Lysanias was tetrarch of Abilene during the fifteenth year of the reign of Tiberius Caesar when the ministry of Jesus began. Two Greek inscriptions have been discovered with the name Lysanias, one which identifies him as tetrarch of Abila, which would support Luke's claim that Lysanias was a tetrarch during the time of Tiberius and Pontius Pilate.

Pontius Pilate

In 1961 a stone inscribed with the name of Pontius Pilate—the man who sentenced Jesus to crucifixion—was discovered in Caesarea, which confirmed that he was prefect (governor) of Judea during the time of Jesus's ministry. More recently, a ring was discovered that almost certainly refers to Pontius Pilate.

Caiaphas

Joseph Caiaphas was the high priest of Judaism in Jerusalem from about AD 18 to 36 (Matt. 26:57–67). In 1990 an ornate ossuary was discovered in Jerusalem with the inscription, "Joseph, son of Caiaphas."

THE HERODS

While we often mention Herod in connection to the Christmas story or Jesus's crucifixion, did you know there are six Herods referenced in the Bible? Here are three for whom we have archaeological evidence:

Herod the Great

Herod the Great was the Herod who sought to kill Jesus when he was a child (Matt. 2). He was a Roman client king of Judea for roughly thirty-seven years (ca. 40–4 BC), although he began ruling from Jerusalem in 37 BC. While there is some scholarly debate, it is likely that the sarcophagus of Herod was discovered at a mausoleum at Herodium.

Herod Antipas

Herod Antipas was a son of Herod the Great. In Luke 3:1, Luke mentions Herod Antipas, the "tetrarch of Galilee." John the Baptist spoke out against the marriage between Antipas and Herodias, for which he was imprisoned and eventually executed at the fortress palace of Machaerus on the northeastern side of the Dead Sea. Ruins of the fortress remain to this day.

King Herod Agrippa

Grandson of Herod the Great, Herod Agrippa had Peter arrested and was eventually struck down by an angel and eaten by worms (Acts 12). Many ancient coins have been discovered bearing the inscription of "Agrippa King," ruler of Judea from AD 41–44.

PLACES

While the people of the Gospels are no longer with us, the land of the ancient Near East certainly is. Of course, many of the towns and cities have new names, and most of the physical structures from the time of Jesus are gone. Yet some of it remains buried beneath the ground or under new structures. What follows is a description of the unearthed evidence for some of the places mentioned in the Gospels.

Bethlehem

The Gospels report that Jesus was born in Bethlehem (Matt. 2:1–6; Luke 2:4–7; John 7:41–42). Archaeological discoveries reveal that Bethlehem was occupied as a town during this time. Church writers of the second and third centuries reported that Jesus was born in a cave in Bethlehem (e.g., Justin Martyr *Dialogue of Trypho* 78). In AD 135 Emperor Hadrian had a shrine for Adonis built over the traditional location of the cave where Jesus was born, which suggests that Roman authorities were aware of the significance of the site for Christians.

Nazareth

Because of the lack of early sources outside the New Testament that reference Nazareth, some scholars have doubted that it existed during the time of Jesus. Yet recent archaeological discoveries have confirmed that a village existed at Nazareth during the first century AD. A tomb inscription indicates the use of Aramaic in Nazareth, and a first-century house has been discovered that was occupied by a family who very likely observed the law of Moses.

Capernaum

A fourth- or fifth-century synagogue made of limestone stands over the foundation of a first-century basalt synagogue, which may have been where Jesus preached (John 6:35–59). Nearby, beneath a fifth-century church, lies an earlier octagonal church that was converted from a first-century house. Evidence suggests this house was used as a house church for early Christians, and many scholars even believe this may have been the house of the apostle Peter.

Pool of Bethesda

In John 5, Jesus heals a lame man on the Sabbath by the pool of Bethesda. In 1888, archaeologists discovered the remains of the pool near St. Anne's Church in Jerusalem. Archaeological investigations have confirmed that the pool has five porticoes, as John described.

Pool of Siloam

In John 9, Jesus heals a blind man and tells him to wash himself in the pool of Siloam. Coins and pottery from the first century, along with a careful excavation, have confirmed the discovery of this pool in southern Jerusalem.

CULTURE

As well as substantiating the historicity of various people and places mentioned in the Gospels, archaeological discoveries have corroborated details about the culture during Jesus's life. This confirms the authenticity of the gospel accounts of first-century events and ways of life.

Pots and Jars

Pots and jars are frequently mentioned in the Gospels as a means of storing and transporting liquids such as water and wine. In 2016 a cave was discovered in Galilee that was used as an ancient workshop for crafting stone pots and jars. This cave is just a mile away from the biblical town of Cana. Many similar ritual stone jars and cups have also been found throughout first-century Judea and Galilee, which clearly indicate Jewish worship because the stone jars were used for ritual purposes.

The "Jesus Boat"

Boats are prominent in the Gospels, whether used for fishing or for transportation. In 1986 an ancient boat was discovered in the Sea of Galilee, dating from around 50 BC to 50 AD. Popularly named the "Jesus Boat," this vessel provides insight into the types of boats Jesus and his disciples used.

Leprosy

Jesus performed many miracles, healing illnesses such as blindness and leprosy. Some skeptics doubted that leprosy existed as an illness in the Middle East during Jesus's time. But carbon dating and DNA testing on first-century skeletal remains have confirmed the existence of leprosy during Jesus's lifetime.

Synagogues

While the Gospels describe Jesus frequently visiting synagogues, many scholars doubted that synagogues existed until after the temple was destroyed in AD 70. However, the remains of multiple synagogues dating before AD 70 have been discovered in Israel, confirming their existence and prominence in Jesus's day. In particular, two synagogues have been discovered in Magdala, the birthplace of Mary Magdalene.

Nazareth Inscription

In the nineteenth century, an inscription of an "edict of Caesar" turned up in Nazareth, in which the emperor, perhaps Claudius, ordered anyone robbing or disturbing tombs to be put to death. It dates between the first century BC and the first century AD. The edict warns against stealing a body with "wicked intent" from a rock tomb sealed with a stone. Because of the location and content of the inscription, some scholars have suggested the Romans issued it in response to the Christian claims that Jesus had risen from the dead. If so, the goal would have been to deter any similar claims.

Burial of Criminals

Some critics have argued that crucified criminals were not buried but were either left on the cross to be eaten by animals or would be removed and tossed into a shallow pit. But in 1968 the bones of a young man named Jehohanan were discovered in a tomb. The ankle was pierced with a seven-inch nail, which contained traces of wood from an olive tree. Forensic evidence showed that the man had been crucified in the first century, proving that some criminals were indeed allowed to be buried. Although archaeological evidence of crucifixion is rare, remains of a twenty-five- to thirty-five-year-old man crucified by the Roman Empire (with a nail hammered through the heel bone) and subsequently buried were more recently discovered in England.

CONCLUSION

Archaeology provides an invaluable resource for investigating the historical Jesus. It not only gives insight into the setting of his life, ministry, and execution but also provides historical corroboration for the Gospel records.

CONCLUSION

While the claim that Jesus is just a copycat of pagan and dying and rising gods is popular on the internet, the truth is that it holds zero merit when the evidence is examined. Upon close examination, we have seen how Jesus's death and resurrection are unlike anything from ancient pagan religions. And it is also highly likely that stories of dying and rising gods were based on Jesus, not the other way around.

Of course, some people will still adamantly adhere to "Jesus mythicism" and maintain that Jesus never existed. But in the words of agnostic New Testament scholar Bart Ehrman, "If that's what you're gonna believe, you just look foolish."[1]

HOW JESUS FULFILLS OLD TESTAMENT PROPHECY

As a skeptic examining the Christian faith, I (Josh) quickly homed in on the claim that Jesus fulfilled prophecy. Refuting this would undermine the uniqueness of Jesus and the reliability of the New Testament. Yet as I probed the evidence, fulfilled prophecy ended up being one of the main reasons I became a Christian. The evidence was (and still is) compelling to me. Allow us to explain in this section.

The New Testament writers establish the messianic credentials of Jesus by referring to his resurrection and to fulfilled messianic prophecy. The prophecies that we find in the Hebrew Old Testament differ in a significant way from those found in the Greco-Roman world. To the Greek or Roman, a prophecy was a specific prediction that anticipated a specific single fulfillment. Although the single-fulfillment form of prophecy is also found in the Hebrew Scriptures, the Hebrew understanding of prophecy was considerably broader. While an Old Testament prophecy might be fulfilled immediately or in a relatively short time frame, it may also point forward to an important long-term fulfillment.

It is important that we keep this in mind as we discuss the value of Old Testament prophecy to establish the messianic credentials of Jesus of Nazareth. The numerous and pervasive instances in the Old Testament of description and detail that correspond to the life of Jesus are like threads in a tapestry that gradually weave together to reveal him as the Messiah. Put another way, the Old Testament can be compared to a jigsaw puzzle. The numerous pieces remain puzzling until they are assembled enough to fill out the intended picture. In the same way, the messianic references in the Old Testament remain puzzling until patient study reveals them as a picture of Jesus Christ. The New Testament is thus the decryption key for unlocking the meaning of the Old Testament Scriptures.

CHAPTER 17

WHAT IS THE IMPORTANCE OF OLD TESTAMENT MESSIANIC PROPHECY?

THROUGHOUT JESUS'S EARTHLY MINISTRY, HE PERFORMED various signs and wonders to confirm his deity. His ultimate miracle was rising from the dead. While a resurrection is a sufficient sign to demonstrate that he is God, Jesus also fulfilled Old Testament prophecy to confirm his identity.

GOD IS THE SOURCE OF PROPHECY

First, it is critical to understand that Old Testament prophecy is more than just wise words of gurus or shamans—it is a message directly from God to his people. Thus, we must remember three important points when discussing prophecy:

1. God is true and reliable in all that he says (Num. 23:19).
2. God accomplishes all that he says (Isa. 46:9–10).
3. God announced his Messiah in Scripture and with acts of power (Isa. 48:3, 5; Rom. 1:2–4).

We value prophecy because it comes from God. If Old Testament prophecy has been fulfilled, what is its value for today?

Old Testament Prophecy Can Strengthen the Faith of Believers

We all have periods of doubt. Even John the Baptist, the prophesied forerunner of the Messiah, had doubts about Jesus. As he sat in jail, he questioned whether Jesus was truly the promised Messiah (Matt. 11:3). Like John, we may find our faith in God wavering based on our circumstances. But what will not change is that Jesus is the long-awaited deliverer who was promised to Israel and the world. Old Testament prophecy reminds us of that.

Messianic prophecy also reminds us that God is in control. God promised the coming of Jesus centuries before he was born in a manger, which encourages us that God's plans always come to fruition.

Old Testament Prophecy Demonstrates That Jesus Is the Messiah

Jesus and the New Testament writers constantly appealed to Old Testament prophecy to convince their listeners that Jesus was the promised Messiah.

Jesus

Jesus was in his hometown synagogue on the Sabbath and read a passage from Isaiah about the coming Messiah. When he was done, he announced to those in attendance, "Today this Scripture has been fulfilled in your hearing" (Luke 4:21 ESV).

The people were astonished at his boldness and authority, with many seeking to kill him for his audacious claim.

After his resurrection, Jesus encountered some of his followers on the road to Emmaus. They did not recognize Jesus, and they were very upset that their leader and friend had been killed. He rebuked them for not understanding that the prophets had foretold that the Messiah would suffer and die. Then, "beginning at Moses and all the Prophets, He expounded to them in all the Scriptures the things concerning Himself" (Luke 24:27). Later, Jesus appeared to his disciples and explained that "all things must be fulfilled which were written in the Law of Moses and the Prophets and the Psalms concerning Me" (v. 44).

Jesus appealed to Old Testament prophecy on many other occasions too: Matt. 5:17; 13:13–14 (cf. Isa. 6:9); 21:42 (cf. Ps. 118:22), 26:56; Mark 13:26 (cf. Dan. 7:13–14); Luke 22:37 (cf. Isa. 53:12); John 5:39–40, 46–47; 15:25 (cf. Pss. 35:19; 69:4).

New Testament Writers

The New Testament writers also referenced the Old Testament Scriptures when discussing Jesus's deity. We see this in the earliest postresurrection sermons in Acts (3:18; 10:43; 13:29; 17:2–3) as well as the "resurrection creed" of 1 Corinthians 15:3–4. Paul began Romans proclaiming that the message of Jesus was "promised before through His prophets in the Holy Scriptures" (Rom. 1:2). And Peter affirmed that the prophets foretold the suffering and glory of Christ (1 Peter 1:10–12) as well as Jesus's sacrifice and priesthood (2:4–6).

Clearly, in the days of Jesus and the disciples, Old Testament prophecy was critical in showing people that Jesus was the promised Messiah.

Old Testament Prophecy Is Important to Evangelism

Prophecy's important role in evangelism wasn't limited to New Testament days—it's important nowadays as well. We have the benefit of the entire Bible to show that Jesus matches the predictions made by the Old Testament prophets. This is a powerful way to show unbelievers that the Bible is God's Word and that Jesus is God.

CONCLUSION

The Old Testament contains numerous prophecies, types, and foreshadowings that were fulfilled in the person of Jesus of Nazareth. One such coincidence may not compel someone to accept that Jesus was the Messiah. But taken together, the numerous fulfillments of Old Testament Scripture form a tapestry, a cumulative case, for the divine inspiration of Scripture and for the messianic credentials of Jesus. This will be our subject of examination over the next few chapters.

CHAPTER 18

DOES THE OLD TESTAMENT FORESHADOW JESUS?

Part 1

IN THE PREVIOUS CHAPTER, WE DISCUSSED WHY IT IS IMPORtant that Jesus fulfilled Old Testament prophecy. Now we will look at the actual prophecies and how Jesus fulfills them.

TYPES AND FORESHADOWINGS

In a narrative text, a detail or element can appear significant enough for a reader to feel it hints at some larger idea while remaining a real part of its own story. Centuries of biblical interpreters have followed the lead of the authors of Scripture, who quote the Old Testament to emphasize and explain a detail they believe points to Christ. The authors of Scripture make these kinds of connections by recognizing a fundamental and theological unity between the element's meaning in the initial narrative and its meaning in the life or work of Christ. The image or other element in the Old Testament is called a type; it foreshadows or prefigures what the New Testament says. In a sense, a type acts like a prophecy. Interpretation using this method must take care to be faithful to the original narrative, letting the meaning arise from the element's function and context in the Old Testament. Let's explore some examples of how the New Testament builds on a type seen in the Old Testament and uses it to show Jesus as its fulfillment.

Christ Our Passover Lamb (Ex. 12:1–28 and 1 Cor. 5:7)

The festival of Passover celebrates God's deliverance of the Israelite people from slavery in Egypt. In the last of the ten plagues imposed because of stubbornness of Pharaoh, the firstborn of every household in his kingdom would die. In every Jewish slave home, the Passover lamb was sacrificed to spare the firstborn from the deadly plague. The lamb's blood would be smeared on the doorposts of their houses as a mark of their faith in God and served as protection from the angel of death. Likewise, Christ is identified in the New Testament as our Passover Lamb, who was sacrificed for us (John 1:29, 36; 1 Cor. 5:7; 1 Peter 1:18–19; Rev. 7:14; 12:11). If we apply his blood to the doorposts of our hearts, so to speak, then the Lord will "pass over" us and no judgment will fall upon us. Other historical details reinforce the validity of Jesus as the Lamb who fulfilled an Old Testament type. The lamb was to be a "male without defect" (Ex. 12:5 NIV), which is a description given of Jesus (1 Peter 1:18–19; Heb. 9:14). None of the lamb's bones were to be broken (Ex. 12:46). Likewise, not a bone of Jesus's body was broken (John 19:32–36).

It is historically attested that Jesus's death coincided with the Jewish Passover feast, on the fifteenth day of Nisan. This seeming coincidence fits much more naturally on the hypothesis that Christianity is true rather than false.

Christ the Lord's Provision (Gen. 22:1–14 and Heb. 11:17–19)

God put Abraham's faith to the ultimate test. Abraham was told to sacrifice his son as a burnt offering. Isaac was identified as his "only son," even though Abraham had another (older) son called Ishmael. But Isaac was the son of the promise (Gen. 15:1–6), making this command especially surprising. It pitted Abraham's love for his son against his faith in God (Heb. 11:17). Isaac carried the wood for his own burnt offering. Similarly, the wood for Christ's sacrifice was laid upon his back when he was required to carry his own cross.

When Isaac asked his father Abraham where the lamb was for the burnt offering, Abraham replied that God would provide it (Gen. 22:7–8). Just as Abraham was about to sacrifice his son, the angel of the Lord stopped him, and Abraham saw a ram caught in a thicket. Abraham sacrificed the ram as a burnt offering instead of his son. Note that the provision was made of a ram rather than a lamb, which suggests that the promised lamb was still to be provided.

Christ Our High Priest and King (Ps. 110:4 and Heb. 7:1–3)

There are a few figures in the Old Testament who had the role of priest and king and who foreshadow Christ. The most prominent is Melchizedek, king of Salem, who shows up in Genesis 14:17–20 and is one of only two in the Bible who simultaneously held the office of priest and king. His name and title are noteworthy. His name means "king of righteousness," and as the king of Salem, which means "peace," he is also the "king of peace." He is given no genealogy, nor do we read of his death. The author of Hebrews interprets this as foreshadowing the eternal priestly rule of our Lord Jesus Christ, who is also both priest and king (Heb. 7:3).

In the book of Hebrews, Jesus is shown to be a priest whose status is far greater than the Levitical priesthood (Heb. 7:1–8:1). The passage cites Psalm 110, which declares Christ to be a "priest forever according to the order of Melchizedek" (Ps. 110:4; Heb. 7:17). Thus, the author of Hebrews declares this psalm to be a prophecy fulfilled in Christ. Jesus quotes Psalm 110:1 when he challenges the Pharisees to reflect on what they think about the Messiah, and Peter quotes that verse in his sermon at Pentecost as a credential for identifying Jesus as the promised Messiah (Matt. 22:41–46; Acts 2:32–36). Overall, the psalm presents a priest-king of a very high order, acting on God's authority. Its reference to Melchizedek, a king of righteousness and peace as well as a mysterious priest, shows an Old Testament type reaching far beyond its original historical context to a fulfillment in Christ.

The Bronze Serpent (Num. 21:8–9 and John 3:14–15)

On their journey out of slavery toward the promised land, the children of Israel murmured against God. As judgment, God sent among them fiery, poisonous serpents. When the Israelites urged Moses to intercede before God for them, God commanded Moses to make a serpent of bronze that would be raised on a pole. Anyone who had been bitten by one of the serpents could look upon the bronze serpent and be delivered from death.

This image typifies the way of salvation revealed by the New Testament. The poison represents God's judgment because of our sin and rebellion against a holy God. The serpent that was lifted up bore the image of that which brought the poison and death, just as Christ bore the nature of humanity to bring healing and redemption. The bitten Israelites exercised faith by looking at the serpent on the pole. No work of righteousness could have saved them from the death that was already working in them. In their act of faith, they experienced not merely healing but also the gift of life. Jesus makes this specific connection in his conversation with Nicodemus when he compares Moses lifting up the serpent in the desert to the Son of Man being lifted up (John 3:14). Just as the Israelites in the desert were saved by looking at the serpent on the pole, eternal life comes to all who "look" at Jesus by believing in him.

The Son of Man (Dan. 7:13–14 and Mark 14:61–62)

Jesus's favorite self-designation in the Gospels is the title Son of Man. During his trial, Jesus connects this title with the image of "coming with the clouds of heaven" (Mark 14:62), drawing our attention to the prophetic text of Daniel 7:13–28. The Son of Man is described here as being given an everlasting dominion over all peoples and is therefore, we submit, the *head* of the saints of the Most High. This exaltation of the Son of Man seems to be the fundamental detail linking both Jesus's frequent use of the name (even at his trial) and the use of the name in the rest of the New Testament (e.g., Rev. 1:13).

MESSIANIC PREDICTIVE PROPHECIES

Aside from messianic types and foreshadowings of the Messiah, the Old Testament also predicted facts about the Messiah that were true of Jesus. We list twelve here:

FACT	OLD TESTAMENT	NEW TESTAMENT
Pre-existent and divine	Isa. 9:6	Col. 1:17; John 8:58; Rev. 1:17; 22:13
A prophet	Deut. 18:18	Matt. 21:11; Luke 7:16; John 4:19; 6:14; 7:40
Of the line of Jesse and the house of David	Isa. 11:1–3	Rom. 1:1–3
Judge	Ezek. 34:20–24	2 Tim. 4:1
King	Ps. 2:6; see also Jer. 23:5; Zech. 9:9	Matt. 21:5; 27:37; John 18:33–38
Special presence of the Holy Spirit	Isa. 11:2	Matt. 3:16–17; 12:17–21; Mark 1:10; Luke 4:15–21, 43; John 1:32
Preceded by messenger	Isa. 40:3; Mal. 3:1	Mark 1:1–3
Ministry to begin in Galilee	Isa. 9:1	Matt. 4:12–17
Ministry of miracles	Isa. 35:5–6	Matt. 9:35
He was to enter the temple	Mal. 3:1	Matt. 21:12
He was to enter Jerusalem on a donkey	Zech. 9:9	Luke 19:35–37
A "light" to the gentiles	Isa. 42:6; 49:5–6	Acts 13:47–48; 26:23; 28:28

CONCLUSION

This chapter has examined types and foreshadowings in the Old Testament that find fulfilment in Jesus as Israel's awaited Messiah, as well as prophecies about him and events in his life. The next chapter will continue exploring Old Testament prophecy.

CHAPTER 19

DOES THE OLD TESTAMENT FORESHADOW JESUS?

Part 2

WE JUST EXPLORED SOME OF THE OLD TESTAMENT PROPHE-
cies fulfilled in Jesus. Let's examine some more here. This
chapter reveals even more ways in which the Old Testament
paves the way for the coming of Jesus. Though none of these
examples considered individually proves that Jesus is the
Messiah, together they are part of a broader cumulative argument for Jesus's Messianic identity.

THE SERVANT SONG OF ISAIAH

One of the most remarkable prophecies concerning the
sufferings and mission of the Messiah is found in Isaiah
52:13–53:12, commonly referred to as one of the Servant
Songs. The passage begins with the servant being "high
and lifted up" and "exalted" (Isa. 52:13 ESV), which recalls
Isaiah's description of Yahweh as sitting on his throne: "I saw
the Lord sitting on a throne, high and lifted up" (Isa. 6:1).
The individual in this text is identified as God's "servant"

throughout the prophecy, which indicates that he would be a prophet or religious leader. The servant's pitiable condition is described in 52:14: "His appearance was so marred, beyond human semblance, and his form beyond that of the children of mankind." Yet according to verse 15, he would influence many nations for good, albeit in a manner typified in the Jewish sacrificial system. Verse 15 also indicates that he would be acknowledged by gentile kings, though his identity had not been hitherto revealed to them.

The text goes on to assert that the servant would be scarcely recognized for who he was (Isa. 53:1–3). In fact, his physical appearance would be so unattractive that the people would not find him desirable (v. 2). The text indicates that he would be despised and rejected and that his life would be marked by sorrow and grief (vv. 3–4). Furthermore, the servant would be accursed by God, though his suffering was for our sakes (vv. 4–5). He would be pierced as well as scourged, though it was not for his own sins, but rather for those of others, which were, in consequence, atoned for (vv. 5–6). His suffering would be voluntary and endured with patience (v. 7). He is even likened to a lamb being led to the slaughter, which carries echoes of Passover. He is described as remarkably silent before his accusers. He would be put on trial, unjustly condemned, sentenced to death, and executed (v. 8). He would be appointed to die with the wicked, and the rich would be involved in his burial, though he was perfectly innocent and his speech was without deceit (v. 9). God, however, would raise him from the dead (v. 10), and through his suffering and intercession many people would be made right with God (vv. 11–12).

It is worth appreciating the context for Isaiah 53, which names what the suffering servant will bring with him: peace, joy, salvation, and the rule of God (Isa. 52:7–10). Echoing Isaiah 40, the text speaks of the Lord himself coming to Zion to redeem his people. The New Testament writers speak of all these blessings as coming through Christ, who is the fulfillment of these prophecies.

THE MESSIAH WOULD BE JEWISH

In Deuteronomy 18:18, God says to Moses, in reference to the Messiah, "I will raise up for them a prophet like you from among their brothers. And I will put my words in his mouth, and he shall speak to them all that I command him" (ESV). This indicates that the Messiah would be Jewish. God also told Abraham that through his offspring all the nations of the earth would be blessed (Gen. 22:18).

THE MESSIAH WOULD BE OF THE LINE OF DAVID

Various texts indicate that the Messiah would be of the line of David. For example, Isaiah 9:7 indicates that he will sit "on the throne of David and over his kingdom" (ESV). Isaiah 11:1 also describes the Messiah as being "a shoot from the stump of Jesse [the father of David]" (ESV).

THE MESSIAH WOULD BE BORN IN BETHLEHEM

According to Micah 5:2, the Messiah would be born in Bethlehem: "But you, O Bethlehem Ephrathah, who are too little to be among the clans of Judah, from you shall come forth for me one who is to be ruler in Israel, whose coming forth is from of old, from ancient days" (ESV).

THE MESSIAH WOULD HAVE GLOBAL INFLUENCE

The Scriptures indicate that though the Messiah would be rejected by his own people (Isa. 53:3–4), he would ultimately bring representatives of all nations to a recognition of the God of Israel (Isa. 42:6; 49:6; 52:15; Dan. 7:14). This is an improbable feat, one uniquely fulfilled by Jesus of Nazareth.

THE CRUCIFIXION

Psalm 22 contains a description of the sufferings of the Messiah that bears striking resemblance to a crucifixion scene. Verses 12–18 say,

> Many bulls encompass me;
>> strong bulls of Bashan surround me;
> they open wide their mouths at me,
>> like a ravening and roaring lion.
>
> I am poured out like water,
>> and all my bones are out of joint;
> my heart is like wax;
>> it is melted within my breast;
> my strength is dried up like a potsherd,
>> and my tongue sticks to my jaws;
>> you lay me in the dust of death.

> For dogs encompass me;
>> a company of evildoers encircles me;
> they have pierced my hands and feet.
> I can count all my bones—
> they stare and gloat over me;
> they divide my garments among them,
>> and for my clothing they cast lots. (ESV)

Dislocation of bones, lack of strength, dehydration, heart failure, and piercing of hands and feet are all apt descriptions of the experience of crucifixion. Part of the humiliation of crucifixion was that the victim would be stripped naked. This comports with the psalmist's description of the dividing of his garments and the casting of lots. The psalmist also appears to portray a public execution event, since people are said to stare and gloat over him.

That Psalm 22 is indeed a messianic text is supported by the fact that the deliverance from death of the individual concerned is said to be occasion for the world's conversion (Ps. 22:27–31). Furthermore, verse 6 says, "But I am a worm and not a man, scorned by mankind and despised by the people" (ESV). This resembles the language of Isaiah 53:3: "He was despised and rejected by men, a man of sorrows and acquainted with grief; and as one from whom men hide their faces he was despised, and we esteemed him not" (ESV).

THE REMOVAL OF THE SCEPTER

Way back in the beginning of the Bible, in Genesis, the patriarch Jacob blessed his sons and their descendants. He told

Judah, "The scepter shall not depart from Judah, nor a law-giver from between his feet, until Shiloh comes; and to Him shall be the obedience of the people" (Gen. 49:10). The word translated "scepter" in this passage means a "tribal staff" or "a ruler's staff." The "tribal staff" of Judah was not to pass away before Shiloh came. For centuries Jewish and Christian commentators alike have taken the word *Shiloh* to be a name of the Messiah, for it means "peace-bringer."

The southern kingdom of Judah was deprived of its national sovereignty for the seventy-year Babylonian captivity. But Judah never lost its "tribal staff" or "national identity" during that time. They still possessed their own lawgivers or judges even while in captivity (Ezra 1:5, 8).

According to Genesis 49:10 and to the Jewish interpreters of the Old Testament, two signs were to take place at the advent of the Messiah:

- Removal of the scepter or identity of Judah
- Suppression of the judicial power

After the return from Babylon, there was no king. The Maccabean princes, who ruled for a time, were of the tribe of Levi. Herod the Great, who had no Jewish blood, succeeded the Maccabean princes and was appointed as an agent of Roman rule. Though the tribe of Judah existed, it provided no kings: the Idumean line of Herod continued to rule, under the authority of Rome.

The power of the Jewish lawgivers was also sharply restricted at the time of Christ, including the loss of the power to pass the death sentence, which was reserved for the Roman

Empire alone. Thus, the prophecy of Jacob to Judah was fulfilled in the time of Christ.

THE GLORY OF THE LORD FILLING THE TEMPLE

Writing during the days of the building of the Second Temple, approximately 520 BC, Haggai prophesied in sweeping terms that the glory of the Lord would fill the temple and bring peace (Hag. 2:6–9). While the verses mention silver and gold, interpreters have noted that this Scripture must refer to more than just physical splendor, as in many ways the Second Temple was inferior to the first. The best explanation is that Jesus the Messiah, the Lord himself, who carried the very presence of God, came to this temple, worked miracles there, and taught the people God's ways. The Prince of Peace visited the temple and, after his resurrection, sent his Spirit to his apostles, who continued working miracles at the temple. In this way, the glory of God filled the Second Temple in a way that was greater than the way he filled the First Temple.

DIVINE VISITATION AT THE TEMPLE BEFORE ITS DESTRUCTION

Multiple Old Testament prophecies testified that the Messiah would come while the temple at Jerusalem was still standing (Ps. 118:26; Dan. 9:26; Hag. 2:7–9; Zech. 11:13; Mal. 3:1). This is of great significance since the temple was destroyed in AD 70 and has never been rebuilt! The passage from Daniel is exact: "After the sixty-two weeks Messiah shall be cut off, but not for Himself; and the people of the prince who is to come shall destroy the city and the sanctuary" (9:26).

The chronological sequence is remarkable:

+ Messiah comes (assumed)
+ Messiah cut off (dies)
+ Destruction of city (Jerusalem) and sanctuary (the temple)

Titus and his army destroyed the temple and city in AD 70; therefore, either the Messiah had already come, or this prophecy was false.

CHAPTER 20

WHAT ARE THE OBJECTIONS TO MESSIANIC PROPHECY?

THROUGHOUT MY LIFE, I (JOSH) HAVE SPOKEN IN HUNDREDS of university classrooms on the identity of Jesus. When I appeal to fulfilled prophecy, a number of common objections arise. Some critics claim that the New Testament writers purposefully shaped their material to match passages in the Old Testament, others claim that they stretched the meanings of obscure references, and others claim that Old Testament references are taken out of context. Let's consider these common objections.

Objection #1: The gospel authors deliberately crafted their biographies of Jesus to make Jesus appear to fulfill the Old Testament Scriptures.

Answer: One response to this objection is to point out the historicity of specific messianic prophecies. For instance, it is incontrovertible that Jesus uniquely brought representatives of all nations to a recognition of the God of Israel, fulfilling Isaiah 49:6. There is also good evidence Jesus was born in Bethlehem, fulfilling Micah 5:2. And there is compelling evidence of the destruction of the temple within a generation of the life and ministry of Jesus, fulfilling Daniel

9:26. These are just a few of the examples that cumulatively challenge the idea that the gospel writers made it appear as if Jesus fulfilled the Old Testament Scriptures. In many cases, we can historically establish that the prophets' predictions came true.

Additionally, there are several reasons to believe that the gospel authors reported Jesus's life and words accurately. They wrote the truth even at risk of persecution, and they did not play to what their audience might expect.

At the time the gospels were written, the Christian church was undergoing considerable persecution. Many Christians were martyred in excruciating and inhumane ways, such as by crucifixion, being burned alive, or being fed to wild animals. Since the gospel writers had nothing obvious to gain from inventing a new religion, and everything to lose, this suggests they recorded what actually happened and what Jesus really said.

Although the gospel authors evidently embraced an elevated Christology (e.g., Jesus is identified as Yahweh in Mark 1:2–3), Jesus himself, in quoted speech, is remarkably cryptic about his self-identity. It seems likely that if the gospel authors had felt themselves at liberty to make things up, Jesus would have been recorded as stressing his own messianic and divine status much more emphatically.

The Jewish understanding of the messianic prophecies emphasized a coming king, so in the time of Jesus the Jews hoped for a messiah who would end the Roman occupation. If the New Testament writers' motivation was to persuade people who longed for a conquering hero, they could have omitted or downplayed the crucifixion to craft a convincing presentation.

But they didn't. Since, instead, they gave it emphasis, their account is clearly truthful and reveals the saving role of the Messiah in a far deeper way.

Objection #2: Old Testament types and foreshadowings are typically stretched and contrived and therefore offer little evidential support for Jesus's messianic credentials.

Answer: It is certainly true that Christians have tended to stretch some examples of Old Testament typology or look for hidden symbolism where there is probably none. In the previous chapters, however, we selected some of the clearest and most profound prophecies. We contend that, taken together, these biblical passages make a compelling cumulative case for Jesus as the Messiah—the Savior anticipated throughout God's revelation in the Old Testament. The close correspondence between details in the life of Jesus and various Old Testament texts can be explained only by either (1) purposeful contrivance or (2) divine orchestration. Because the New Testament authors wrote courageously to record real history accurately, the weight of detailed evidence leans toward divine orchestration as the best explanation.

Objection #3: The gospel authors took various Old Testament texts out of context to prove that Jesus was the Messiah.

Answer: It's true that the authors of the New Testament applied some texts from the Old Testament to the Messiah when, in their original context, those texts do not directly apply to the Messiah. However, in many cases, when we study them more closely, we discover that they reveal insights that connect both texts, revealing a multilayered meaning.

Many New Testament writers quoted Old Testament words and set them in a new context, as did other Jewish, and later, Christian, commentators on the Old Testament. Let us consider one common example of a passage that the New Testament is frequently alleged to quote out of context.

Matthew quotes Hosea 11:1 toward the beginning of his gospel: "Out of Egypt I called My son" (Matt. 2:15). Matthew states that Jesus's return from the flight to Egypt after the death of King Herod "was to fulfill what the Lord had spoken by the prophet" (ESV). In the original context of Hosea 11:1, the "son" called out of Egypt is in fact the nation of Israel, called out of Egyptian slavery. However, when we see what Matthew is attempting to do in quoting this text, it becomes clear that Hosea is not being quoted out of context at all. One theme of Matthew's gospel is that Jesus is the true Israel—that is to say, Christ succeeds where Israel failed. This is seen, for instance, in Matthew 4:1–4, where Jesus is led into the wilderness for forty days and forty nights to fast and be tested. When the devil tempts Jesus to turn stones into bread, he quotes Deuteronomy 8:3: "Man shall not live by bread alone, but by every word that comes from the mouth of God." The context of this text is Israel's wilderness wandering for forty years, during which time the people hungered and were tested. Matthew draws a similar parallel between Jesus and Israel in Matthew 2:15, where Jesus is said to fulfill Hosea 11:1—just as Israel was called out of Egypt, so likewise is the Messiah. There is even a parallel between Herod the Great's slaughter of the infants of Bethlehem and Pharaoh's slaughter of the Hebrew infants in Egypt. The exodus is said to have taken place "by night" (Ex. 12:29–42). The phrase "by night" is also used in Matthew 2:14.

Thus, Matthew is not interpreting Hosea 11:1 as a messianic prophecy. Rather, he is drawing a parallel between the history of Israel and the life of the Messiah.

CONCLUSION

THE IMPORTANCE OF OLD TESTAMENT PROPHECY IN DEMONstrating the identity of Jesus of Nazareth cannot be overstated. The chances of any one person fulfilling just a handful of prophecies are extremely slim, let alone *all* of them. But if you still need convincing that Jesus is the promised Messiah and Son of God, we will look at the evidence for Jesus's resurrection, an event that confirms Jesus's deity.

EVIDENCE FOR THE RESURRECTION OF JESUS

WHEN I (JOSH) BEGAN INVESTIGATING CHRISTIANITY, I knew that if I could disprove the resurrection, the entire Christian faith would come crashing down. *Everything rests on Jesus rising from the dead.* As Paul made clear in 1 Corinthians 15, if Jesus has not risen, then Christianity is false. End of story.

Before we get to the evidence and respond to common objections, let's begin with whether miracles are possible. After all, if miracles are not possible, then there must be some naturalistic explanation for why the apostles began preaching that Jesus had risen. We explored the possibility of miracles in our discussion of the virgin birth, but we need to go deeper before considering the ultimate miracle that points to the truth of Christianity—the resurrection.

CHAPTER 21

ARE MIRACLES POSSIBLE?

YEARS AGO I (SEAN) WAS SPEAKING WITH AN ATHEIST, A PHD student in physics. He asked me, "How can you believe in miracles like the resurrection of Jesus? Hasn't science shown that when people die, they stay dead?" I responded by saying, "You're right, science has shown that under normal conditions, dead people stay dead. But the Christian claim is that Jesus rose supernaturally—that is, that God has acted in history by raising Jesus from the dead. If there really is a God who created the world and designed its laws, then the norm of dead people staying dead can't restrict God from supernaturally raising his Son."

Here's the simple point that must be repeated: *If God possibly exists, then miracles are possible.* Some skeptics want to dismiss the possibility of miracles unless God's existence can first be demonstrated. But this is backward. It is not up to the theist to prove God's existence, for if the existence of God is not impossible, then miracles are at least possible. To reject miracle claims outright, the skeptic needs to prove that God does not exist. But the nonexistence of God has never been shown. Rather, since the mid-nineteenth century, God's nonexistence has often been *assumed*. Not only has God's nonexistence not been demonstrated, but there are also good reasons to believe that God *does* exist.

THE CHARACTERISTICS OF MIRACLES

Since the nature of miracles is often misunderstood today, here's a closer look at what constitutes a miracle.

Miracles Are Supernatural Events

Miracles are supernatural events, not events produced by finite power. Some agent external to the world brings about the event we call a miracle.

Miracles Are Rare

Miracles do not happen often. They are connected to God's supreme oversight of human history. We shouldn't be presumptuous or demand a miracle. If miracles were frequent, they might be predictable. If they were predictable, then what would distinguish a miracle from the normal course of nature? The Bible even describes periods when miracles were particularly rare (see 1 Sam. 3:1).

Miracles Are Unpredictable

God is a free agent, and there is no conclusive formula that allows us to determine when, where, or how a miracle will occur. Miracles are unpredictable, and finite beings can't always predict the activity of a divine being. God is under no compulsion to perform a miracle, so if God brings about a miracle, it's due to his initiative and will. To make this point, philosopher Timothy McGrew invites people to imagine encountering a cabin in the forest that initially appears to be uninhabited. But upon inspection, you discover a cup of hot tea on the table. The hypothesis that the cabin is uninhabited would not lead you to predict the presence of the hot tea. The point of this imaginary scenario is that even though we cannot predict when miracles will occur, they nonetheless are of evidential value in confirming special divine action.[1]

Miracles Can't Be Tested with the Scientific Method

The unpredictability of miracles means we can't test them with the scientific method. The scientific method requires a hypothesis, a controlled experiment, and a conclusion. Since God is sovereign, we cannot test his actions as we can other events in nature. But this doesn't mean we can't investigate the miraculous. In some cases, scientific tools may help. For instance, science could be used to verify that someone had a medical condition, such as a tumor, and then that tumor is gone. Miracles occur within history, so they can be investigated like other events in the past.

Miracles Always Promote Good and Glorify God Alone

Miracles are not like magic tricks for show but have the distinct purpose of glorifying God. Since God is good, miracles are meant to promote good, and God alone deserves the glory for miracles.

Miracles Are Not Contradictions

God can't create square circles or married bachelors because they are logical impossibilities. But there's nothing logically contradictory about some events that are not physically possible. For example, it's physically impossible to walk on water. But there's nothing logically contradictory about it, and thus God *can* make it happen if he desires.

THE PURPOSE OF MIRACLES

To provide us a context in which to examine miracles, we also need to explore the purpose of miracles. Miracles are for more than amazement. They serve God's purposes in two primary ways. First, they confirm a message from God. Miracles are a sign of the truthfulness of God's word. Second, miracles confirm a messenger from God. In John 3:2, Nicodemus says of Jesus, "Rabbi, we know that you are a teacher who has come from God. For no one could perform the signs you are doing if God were not with him" (NIV). Many people followed Jesus because of the signs and wonders he performed.

MODERN MIRACLES

"If miracles are possible," says the skeptic, "then why don't they still happen?" That's a fair question. If miracles happened nowadays, that would certainly give added support to the biblical accounts of miracles. In his book *A Simple Guide to Experience Miracles*, Christian philosopher J. P. Moreland describes and verifies a few modern-day miracles.

J. P. gave a talk on the supernatural to a group of students. One student, David, had been born legally blind in one eye, able only to vaguely distinguish dark and light. Another student, Elise, was inspired by J. P.'s talk and decided to pray for the healing of a few students, including David. The next day, David found that he was able to see perfectly fine with the eye in which he had been legally blind. J. P. received email confirmation from a ministry leader as well as from Elise and David about this healing account.[2]

Nathan was diagnosed with GERD (gastroesophageal reflux disease) at the age of thirteen. After suffering with it for nine years, he sought out surgical correction for his condition. Nathan learned he would need a series of five surgeries and require medication for the rest of his life. While Nathan was at a Bible study meeting, the guest speaker suddenly announced there was a person present who suffered from GERD. Nathan identified himself as that person, and the speaker prayed for Nathan's healing. Nathan was instantly healed and has not suffered a single incident since that meeting. He also received confirmation of his healing from his doctor.[3]

J. P. himself has also received healing of an illness. He had caught a bad virus and was left with severe laryngitis that would take seven to ten days to heal. J. P. was distraught, as he had courses to teach and a speaking engagement that week. But when his wife informed his church elders of his laryngitis, they prayed for J. P.'s healing. As the men prayed, J. P. felt warmth in his chest and throat flowing from the elder's hand, and J. P. was completely healed.[4]

J. P. is not the only scholar who has documented and verified accounts of the miraculous. New Testament scholar Craig Keener has written a thoroughly researched two-volume study of modern-day miracles entitled *Miracles*, as well as a popular-level version of this study, *Miracles Today*. Miracles do still happen today. And because they occur today, we can be all the more confident that they occurred in biblical times as well.

CONCLUSION

Are miracles possible? Again, your answer to this question most likely depends on your worldview. If you believe that the natural world is all that exists and you accept only natural explanations to events, no matter how unlikely, then you already have a philosophical presupposition against miracles. But this is an assumption, not a proof. If it's possible that God exists, then it is certainly possible that this God may choose to intervene in the regular course of nature in a unique way. After all, if God can create the universe and all its laws, then certainly God can violate those laws if he wants. Miracles are most definitely possible.

With this in mind, let's examine the evidence for the most audacious miracle claim in human history: the resurrection of Jesus.

CHAPTER 22

WHAT ARE THE FACTS OF THE RESURRECTION?

When I (Josh) first examined the resurrection, I was surprised to learn about *any* positive evidence for the life, death, and appearances of Jesus. As I continued to study the historical evidence—which is considerably stronger now—I became convinced that the resurrection is the best explanation for the known facts. We will present some of the facts about the death of Jesus and the facts about the time after Jesus's death.

PRERESURRECTION FACTS

In looking at events just prior to Jesus's resurrection, we'll consider the way in which Jesus died and the way he was buried.

Jesus Died by Crucifixion

There are three types of sources for the evidence regarding the manner in which Jesus died. They include the New Testament, scientific research, and scholars critical of Christianity's truth claims. Here are some important points regarding Jesus's death by crucifixion:

First, the Gospels and other New Testament documents attest that Jesus died by crucifixion (Matt. 27:35–50; Mark 15:27–37; Luke 23:33–46; John 19:23–30; Gal. 2:20).

Second, science confirms that what Jesus endured during and prior to his crucifixion would certainly have killed him. In an article in the peer-reviewed *Journal of the American Medical Association*, William D. Edwards, Wesley J. Gabel, and Floyd E. Hosmer noted that Jesus's death would have occurred from many factors, such as "hypovolemic shock, exhaustion asphyxia, and perhaps acute heart failure," and possibly even "fatal cardiac arrhythmia."[1] To confirm whether Jesus was dead, a solder pierced Jesus's side with a spear. Both blood and water came from the wound, which is precisely what would have happened if Jesus were dead (John 19:31–34).

Third, as discussed in chapter 2, extrabiblical writers wrote that Jesus died, including non-Christians such as Tacitus and Josephus. And even scholars who are critical of Christianity accept Jesus's death by crucifixion. Here is just a sample:

Jesus' death as a consequence of crucifixion is indisputable.[2]

That he was crucified is as sure as anything historical can ever be, since both Josephus and Tacitus . . . agree with the Christian accounts on this basic fact.[3]

The crucifixion of Jesus by the Romans is one of the most secure facts we have about his life. Whenever anyone writes a book about the historical Jesus, it is really (really,

really) important to see if what they say about his public ministry can make sense of his death.[4]

I take it absolutely for granted that Jesus was crucified under Pontius Pilate. Security about the *fact* of the crucifixion derives not only from the unlikelihood that Christians would have invented it but also from the existence of two early and independent non-Christian witnesses to it, a Jewish one from 93–94 C.E. and a Roman one from the 110s or 120s C.E.[5]

Why would these critics so confidently affirm Jesus's death by crucifixion? The simple reason is that the historical evidence is so strong. Additionally, crucifixion was the most shameful way to die. It certainly would have been a poor way to start a new religion by inventing a claim that the founder had been stripped, tortured, and publicly dishonored. The evidence is compelling that Jesus died by crucifixion.

Jesus Was Buried

Just as with the crucifixion, Jesus's burial is described in the Gospels (Matt. 27:59–60; Mark 15:46; Luke 23:53; and John 19:38–40). Some critics doubt whether Jesus was buried in a tomb, as Romans did not allow crucified people to be buried. But as noted in chapter 16, remains of crucified people have been found buried in tombs. Also, the Romans did allow the Jews to follow their own customs, such as burying executed criminals. All four gospels report that Jesus was buried in a tomb, and there is no evidence to the contrary. Although Paul does not explicitly mention the tomb, he mentions the death, burial, and resurrection of Jesus (1 Cor. 15:3–4). The burial of Jesus in a tomb is the best explanation of the known facts.

POSTRESURRECTION FACTS

We've explored the facts of Jesus's death and burial. Now we discuss the facts *after* Jesus's death, which include the empty tomb and his appearances.

Jesus's Tomb Was Empty

First, it is important to note that a significant majority of scholars accept the empty tomb. All but one of the naturalistic theories we plan to address in subsequent chapters implicitly acknowledge the fact of the empty tomb since they attempt to explain the disappearance of the body. For instance, the claim that the disciples stole the body *assumes* that the tomb was not occupied. The only alternate theory that does not fit this profile is the hallucination theory, which seeks to explain the postmortem appearances, not an empty tomb.

Women Were First

The first people to discover the empty tomb were women (Matt. 28:1–10; Mark 16:1–11; Luke 24:1–10; John 20:1–18). Why is this important? In Jesus's day, women had low social status and were not considered credible witnesses. Their testimony was not considered as valuable as a man's testimony. If the disciples were inventing the story of the empty tomb, why include women as the first witnesses? It is deeply counterintuitive and suggests that the disciples believed women really discovered the empty tomb.

Multiple Attestation

The empty tomb is attested by multiple New Testament sources (Matt. 28:11–15; Mark 16:1–8; Luke 24:1–12; John 20:11–18). Aside from these explicit references, speeches in Acts 13 (v. 29) and the creed in 1 Corinthians 15:3–5 presuppose that Jesus's tomb was empty.

Jewish Response

The Jewish leaders accused the disciples of stealing Jesus's body (Matt. 28:11–15). This is significant because you don't accuse someone of stealing something that isn't missing. The Jewish leaders wouldn't need an explanation for the disappearance of the body if the tomb were still occupied.

OBJECTION: WHY DIDN'T PAUL MENTION THE EMPTY TOMB?

1 Corinthians 15 contains one of the earliest and most important statements regarding the resurrection. While the passage mentions Jesus's death, burial, and appearances (1 Cor. 15:3–7), it says nothing about the empty tomb. Critics claim that if the tomb were empty, Paul would have mentioned it. Does this cause a problem for Christians? Not at all. The resurrection passage in 1 Corinthians 15 is intended as a creedal, confessional statement of faith, not a strict historical narrative like other authors, such as Luke, included in their resurrection

accounts. Thus, we shouldn't be surprised that 1 Corinthians 15 omits specific mention of the empty tomb. We should *expect* the omission given the nature of creedal summaries that contained only the most important facts: Christ died, was buried, was raised, and appeared. This summary clearly implies an empty tomb.

Jesus Appeared

In at least twelve distinct instances, Jesus appeared to individuals or groups of people after his death, burial, and resurrection:

1. Mary Magdalene (John 20:11–18)
2. Women leaving the tomb (Matt. 28:8–10)
3. Emmaus disciples (Luke 24:13–35)
4. Simon Peter (Luke 24:34; see also 1 Cor. 15:5)
5. Disciples without Thomas (Luke 24:36–43)
6. Disciples with Thomas (John 20:24–29)
7. Disciples at the Sea of Galilee (Tiberias) (John 21:1–2)
8. Disciples on a mountain in Galilee (Matt. 28:16–17)
9. Disciples (Luke 24:50–52)
10. Five hundred believers (1 Cor. 15:6)
11. James, Jesus's half-brother (1 Cor. 15:7)
12. Paul, an enemy of the church (Acts 9:3–6)

If Jesus was indeed resurrected, then it was a physical Jesus that the disciples saw and interacted with in some fashion. It was radically different from the disembodied continuation after death that appears in other ancient documents known in the Greek and Roman worlds (e.g., Plato, Homer, and Virgil). In contrast, the New Testament insists in a bold and historically reliable way that Jesus rose into a physically transformed body. He was not just a spirit, nor was the resurrection a metaphor.

OBJECTION: WERE THE APPEARANCES VISIONS?

Some critics attribute the resurrection appearances to mere visions or some form of immaterial "resurrection." They argue that the claims of physical appearances were legendary accretions added to the story later. But this objection has some problems.

Luke cared very much about accuracy: he declares his intention for writing about Jesus—to offer certainty for his reader, having searched, investigated, and prepared an orderly account (Luke 1:1–4). He records in Luke 24:36–43 that "Jesus himself stood among" his disciples (NIV), but they believed he was a ghost. To prove he wasn't a ghost, Jesus told them to touch his hands and feet. Jesus also ate some fish in front of them, confirming that he was fully present and not just a spirit. Jesus wanted his disciples to know he was physically resurrected from the dead, and Luke wanted his readers to know this as well.

We must also look at the evidence itself. Here are a few important points:

1. First Corinthians 15:3–8 is early testimony by Paul that he saw the risen Christ. Paul presents his experience of Jesus alongside the list of earlier appearances of Jesus to the apostles and five hundred. Given that

Luke was a traveling companion of Paul, it would be surprising if his understanding of the apostolic claim concerning the resurrection differed from Paul's account here.

2. As mentioned earlier, the first people to see the risen Christ were women. Given the low credibility of women as witnesses in first-century Judaism, it seems unlikely that the gospel writers would invent this type of story.

3. The resurrection reports are very reserved compared with later apocryphal gospels. While there are dramatic events in the gospel accounts, they lack the detailed, fanciful explanations of the resurrection that we find in these apocryphal accounts. For example, in the *Gospel of Peter*, the guards witness the tomb open, and three men come out with two of their heads reaching to the sky. A cross follows them out and speaks in response to a voice from the heavens.

CONCLUSION

Despite the evidence for the resurrection—which we have just summarized here—some people are not convinced. What are the most common naturalistic explanations that some people think better explain the origin of the Christian faith? We will explore that question next.

CHAPTER 23

TWO ALTERNATIVE EXPLANATIONS FOR THE RESURRECTION

IN MY CLASS ON THE RESURRECTION, I (SEAN) OFTEN HAVE students consider various naturalistic hypotheses that attempt to account for belief in the resurrection. Some of these can be found on the internet and others in academic journals. Their job is to analyze the strengths and weaknesses of each theory to see if any can account for the known facts. Examining the theories one by one, they notice an emerging trend: While various theories can account for *some* of the facts, no known naturalistic theory can account for *all* the facts. Keep this in mind as we examine some alternate theories about the resurrection of Jesus in this chapter and the next.

ALTERNATE THEORY #1: APPARENT DEATH THEORY

The apparent death theory (sometimes referred to as the swoon theory) posits that Jesus did not die on the cross, but only *appeared* to die. Although widely rejected by scholars, the swoon theory shows up frequently online and occasionally in academic circles.

Although there are different nuances, here's the basic theory: After being removed from the cross, Jesus was placed in Joseph of Arimathea's tomb while unconscious but still alive. After several hours he revived in the coolness of the tomb, arose, freed himself from burial wrappings and the sealed tomb, and made his way back to his disciples to declare himself the risen Lord, the conqueror and defeater of death. This theory is very recent in historical terms, emerging in the late 1700s and evolving through the late 1800s spread by various liberal German theologians. A modern version of this theory was popularized in the 1965 book *The Passover Plot* by Hugh Schonfield.

RESPONSE TO APPARENT DEATH THEORY

Since 1835 the scholarly community has almost entirely rejected the idea that Jesus survived crucifixion and faked his resurrection. Here's the simple reason: the apparent death theory fails to account for the facts:

Crucifixion Results in Death

The evidence—both historical and medical—argues against the possibility that Jesus survived crucifixion. There are at least twelve reasons for confidence in the biblical account that Jesus died on the cross:

1. The nature of his injuries—whipping, beating, lack of sleep, a crown of thorns, and his collapse on the way to his crucifixion while carrying the cross—were life-endangering in themselves. The nature of crucifixion virtually guarantees death from asphyxiation.

2. The piercing of Jesus's side, from which came "blood and water" (John 19:34), indicating serum separated from clotted blood, gives medical evidence that Jesus had already died.

3. Jesus said he was dying while on the cross: "Father, into your hands I commit my spirit" (Luke 23:46 NIV). John writes that Jesus "gave up His spirit" (John 19:30).

4. The Roman soldiers, who were trained executioners, were charged to make sure that he died. Even though it was customary for soldiers to speed death by breaking the legs of the victims, they did not break Jesus's legs, for their examination determined that he was already dead (John 19:33).

5. Before giving the body to Joseph for burial, Pilate summoned the centurion to make sure Jesus had actually died (see Mark 15:44–45).

6. Jesus's body was wrapped in about a hundred pounds of cloth and spices and placed in a sealed tomb until the third day (John 19:39–40). If Jesus had not died from his previous torture, he would have died in the tomb from lack of food, water, and medical treatment. And if for some reason he didn't, how would he have escaped the linens without help?

7. It is unlikely that the disciples would invent a crucifixion story, since it was such a shameful death, if it were not true.

8. Non-Christian historians from the first and second centuries, such as Tacitus and Josephus, recorded the death of Jesus of Nazareth (see chapter 2).

9. The earliest Christian writers after the time of Christ, such as Polycarp and Ignatius, verified his death by crucifixion on the cross as well.

10. Given his traumatized physical condition, Jesus would have found it extremely difficult, if not impossible, to roll the stone back from the entrance of the tomb, especially from inside the tomb, as there would be no way to obtain leverage against the stone to roll it out of the way (Matt. 27:60).

11. If Jesus were to succeed in rolling away the stone, he would have had to escape without alerting the guards. Whether the guards had fallen asleep, as the story goes (Matt. 28:13), or they were wide awake, Jesus would not be likely to get away from them given his poor physical condition.

12. Even if Jesus had recovered enough to escape the tomb (and the guards!), he certainly would have been in terrible condition. If Jesus had come to the disciples in the state this theory requires, they would not have viewed him as their risen Lord or as someone who had conquered death.

Considering what we know from scientific medical diagnosis, archaeology, and historical documentation, it is highly improbable that Jesus could have survived Roman crucifixion at the hands of trained executioners. The death of Jesus is far and away the best explanation of the facts.

ALTERNATE THEORY #2: THEFT THEORY

The oldest of the naturalistic alternative theories, the theft theory, comes in different forms. The first form is that the disciples stole the body from the sealed and guarded tomb and then conspired to falsely teach that Jesus had been resurrected. The second form is that grave robbers stole the body. Then, when Jesus's followers discovered the tomb empty, they believed Jesus rose from the dead.

This theory originates back to the time of the resurrection itself. Matthew was the first to record it (28:11–15):

> Now while they were going, behold, some of the guard came into the city and reported to the chief priests all the things that had happened. When they had assembled with the elders and consulted together, they gave a large sum of money to the soldiers, saying, "Tell them, 'His disciples came at night and stole Him away while we slept.' And if this comes to the governor's ears, we will appease him and make you secure." So they took the money and did as they were instructed; and this saying is commonly reported among the Jews until this day.

RESPONSE TO THEFT THEORY

The theory that the disciples (or someone else) stole the body fails for several reasons.

Conspiracy by the Disciples

The theory that Jesus's disciples stole the body rests on the assumption that the disciples deliberately conspired with one another to steal the body and then make up a false story that Jesus had risen from the dead. But conspiracies tend to fall apart because someone breaks down under pressure and betrays their coconspirators. This did not happen with the disciples. Rather, they spent their entire lives preaching about the resurrection, built an entire movement around it, and were willing to suffer and die for it.

Unknown Thieves

The theory that someone other than the disciples stole the body faces the same issues surrounding the notion of the disciples' conspiracy. An empty tomb alone would not have convinced Paul, persecutor of Christians, or James, the brother of Jesus, that Jesus rose from the dead. They would have been rightly suspicious. Upon seeing the empty tomb, Mary Magdalene did not conclude that Jesus was risen but that someone had stolen the body. It was not the empty tomb alone that convinced people that Jesus had risen but also his postresurrection appearances.

The Disciples' Lack of Courage

The disciples were scared and in hiding and would not have wanted to take on a sealed and guarded tomb since they were probably afraid of suffering the same fate Jesus had suffered: crucifixion. Remember that the disciples ran away during his arrest, as Jesus predicted (Matt. 26:31, 55–56). Even Peter, though he tried to summon up the courage to follow Jesus into the courtyard, ended up denying Jesus three times (John 13:36–38; 18:15–18, 25–27).

These were not the actions of a group of followers bent on standing up to soldiers guarding a tomb. All the evidence we have indicates they were confused and afraid.

Resurrection Not Expected by Either Gentiles or Jews

As noted earlier, resurrection was not the first thing the disciples concluded when discovering the empty tomb. They immediately jumped to naturalistic conclusions, just as any modern person would. Consider various responses given to the empty tomb:

- Someone moved the body (John 20:2).
- The gardener moved the body (John 20:13–15).
- The women were accused of speaking nonsense, and the men did not believe them (Luke 24:1–11).
- The body was stolen (Matt. 28:11–15).

Neither gentiles nor Jews expected a bodily resurrection of the Messiah. It was an entirely new concept. A dramatic event must have caused their new belief.

The idea that the disciples would somehow summon the courage to come out of hiding, confront an armed guard, steal the body of their leader, concoct a story of a resurrection, and then base an entire movement on Jesus's resurrection and celebrate him as a risen Lord is extremely far-fetched.

Ironically, this theory has one surprise benefit: the religious leaders tacitly acknowledged that the tomb was known and was empty. Otherwise, why invent a story of a stolen body?

CONCLUSION

These two theories unsuccessfully use naturalistic explanations to make sense of the resurrection data. Because many proponents of these theories are committed to a naturalistic worldview, they contort the known historical facts about Jesus. The next chapter explores three more theories.

THREE MORE ALTERNATIVE EXPLANATIONS FOR THE RESURRECTION

IN THE PREVIOUS CHAPTER, WE EXAMINED TWO ALTERNATE explanations of the resurrection data. Let's examine three more here.

ALTERNATE THEORY #3: HALLUCINATION HYPOTHESIS

The hallucination hypothesis states that perhaps Jesus's followers did see him after his crucifixion, but what they saw was just a vision or a hallucination. The disciples had a lot of guilt and grief, so to relieve the tension, their psychological states could have caused them to see Jesus when he wasn't bodily present.

RESPONSE TO HALLUCINATION HYPOTHESIS

While the hallucination hypothesis is commonly held among academics, it has considerable weaknesses. There are five reasons why hallucinations are a poor explanation for the resurrection data:

1. Many people saw Christ appear.
2. They saw Christ individually, not together.
3. Christ did not appear just once but several times.
4. People did not just see him but also touched him, talked to him, and ate with him.
5. The hallucination theory cannot explain the empty tomb.

Group Hallucinations Lack Scientific Support

It should be noted that scientific hallucination studies lack data on group hallucination phenomena. Why? A hallucination is an internal mental event without an external stimulus. Given the lack of a shared external stimulus, it is highly unlikely that multiple people would experience the same hallucination. It is as unlikely as people sharing the same exact dream.

Individual hallucinations are real, but group hallucinations are entirely different. We are not aware of any documented scientific evidence to support the idea of group hallucinations, much less that the disciples and Jesus's other followers were hallucinating in this case.

Recently, I (Sean) interviewed two leading medical doctors on the hallucination hypothesis, Dr. Harold Koenig and Dr. Craig Fowler.[1] Dr. Fowler noted that multisensory hallucinations are very rare, and yet the postresurrection experiences with Jesus involved multiple senses, not just sight.[2] John 21 notes that there were seven disciples who encountered the risen Jesus at the same time. According to the disciples' likely ages at the time of their alleged encounter with Jesus (19–30) and taking only two senses into account—hearing and sight—there is an 0.7 percent chance each one experienced a hallucination. The probability of these seven men having the same hallucination of Jesus at the same time is 0.7 percent raised to the seventh power ((.007) x (.007) x (.007) x (.007) x (.007) x (.007) x (.007)), which is 0.00000000000082354%.[3] This, Dr. Fowler states, is "basically impossible."[4]

Note that this is just one of the resurrection appearances and accounts for only two of the five senses. Jesus also ate with his disciples and invited them to touch him. He appeared to multiple people over many days, with one account recording an appearance to over five hundred people. Considering all these factors, the probability that Jesus's appearances were mere hallucinations is statistically impossible.

The doctors clarified that shared *delusions* are possible among people with strong emotional ties who manifest delusional behavior.[5] But a delusion is different from a hallucination. Dr. Koenig defined a delusion as a "fixed false belief,"[6] which is much different from the simple hallucinatory experiences some groups of people have or the intimate interactions the disciples shared with Jesus over multiple days. A delusion is a *belief*, while a hallucination is an *experience*. Both shared hallucinations and shared delusions are extremely unlikely in the case of the disciples of Jesus.

The lack of scientific evidence for group hallucinations and the unlikeliness of individuals having identical, subjective hallucinations renders the hallucination theory implausible. It seems far more reasonable and plausible that the disciples had real-life experiences with the risen Jesus. There was an external referent (the physical body and person of Jesus) to which they could all attribute a shared experience, rather than flimsy subjective hallucinations lacking any such community event. Moreover, those best in a position to have charged the disciples with hallucinations would have been the high priests, but instead they accused the disciples with theft of the body. This indicates that the high priests must have investigated and found the body to be missing and knew that claiming the disciples hallucinated would not have fit the facts.

ALTERNATE THEORY #4: WRONG TOMB THEORY

The wrong tomb theory holds that those who went to the tomb Sunday morning to pay their respects to Jesus went to the wrong tomb. When they found it empty, they mistook this for evidence of Jesus's resurrection.

RESPONSE TO WRONG TOMB THEORY

We see five major problems with this theory:

1. Even if the disciples went to the wrong tomb, this does not account for their belief that they had *seen* the risen Jesus.
2. The Gospels state that the empty tomb convinced no one except John. Mary concluded that the gardener stole the body. The disciples did not believe upon seeing the empty tomb, but rather were confused.
3. The wrong tomb theory cannot account for the conversion of Paul. He converted based on his belief that he had seen the risen Jesus, not on an empty tomb.
4. An empty tomb alone would not have convinced the skeptic James. Like Paul, James saw the risen Jesus.

5. The evidence suggests that the tomb's location was known because a well-known man, Joseph of Arimathea, buried Jesus in his own tomb. If the burial by Joseph was an invention, then we might expect ancient critics to state that Joseph denied this version of the story. Or the critics could have denied the existence of Joseph if he had been a fictitious character.

For these reasons, and many more, the wrong tomb theory should be abandoned.

ALTERNATE THEORY #5: FAMILY TOMB THEORY

In 2007 the alleged discovery of Jesus's family tomb was a media sensation. The family tomb theory, or Talpiot tomb theory, claims that Jesus was reburied in the family tomb at Talpiot, a few kilometers south of Jerusalem, after spending the Sabbath buried in Joseph of Arimathea's tomb. The discovery of this tomb was so significant that it generated a book and a documentary, *The Lost Tomb of Jesus*, produced by James Cameron, award-winning director of *Titanic* and *Avatar*, and directed by Simcha Jacobovici, host of the Discovery Channel's *The Naked Archaeologist*. The discovery of Jesus's tomb with his bones in it would certainly discredit the resurrection and bring an end to Christianity as we know it.

The Talpiot tomb is claimed to be the family tomb of Jesus of Nazareth. It is further claimed to be his final resting place after a rushed burial on the day of his death, done in order not to violate the Sabbath by handling and burying a corpse after the Sabbath began at sundown. According to this view, Joseph of Arimathea's tomb was temporary, and Jesus's body was moved prior to the women coming to Joseph's tomb to complete the burial process, which would explain why they discovered Jesus's tomb empty. The theory does not tell us who moved the body for reburial.

How did the Talpiot tomb come to be linked with Jesus of Nazareth and his family? And why is it thought to have been Jesus's final resting place? After all, this tomb had originally been excavated in 1980, twenty-seven years before the media frenzy. An ossuary in the excavated tomb contained the inscription "Jesus, son of Joseph." But the original archaeologists dismissed its alleged significance given the popularity of the names Jesus and Joseph in the Palestinian region during its time. However, the team did not consider inscriptions on the other ossuaries in the tomb that allegedly refer to Mary Magdalene and Matthew (the name of one of the twelve disciples).

RESPONSE TO FAMILY TOMB THEORY

This theory has a number of problems. First, some experts say that the primary inscription does not contain the name "Jesus," claiming it is a different name. If this is true, the whole theory collapses. Also, it is doubtful that "Mariamne" refers to Mary Magdalene. The tomb contains no Christian inscriptions and was not venerated, which it likely would have been if it were Jesus's family tomb. Given how popular the names Jesus, Mary, and Joseph were among Jews in first-century Palestine, the presence of these names in a family tomb is not surprising. Further, Matthew was not a family member of Jesus. Why would a disciple from a different family be buried in the family tomb of Jesus? Finally, since Jesus's family had no connections to Jerusalem, he would likely have been buried in Galilee along with other family members.

All of this taken together paints a rather bleak picture for the Talpiot tomb theory. It seems to set aside real, honest scholarship to garner television ratings and book sales. Given the problems with this theory, scholars across the ideological spectrum have denounced the Talpiot tomb theory.

CONCLUSION

While there are more naturalistic theories than we've considered here, they all share one common failure: *an inability to account for all the known facts.* The various theories have to ignore certain facts or offer a speculative explanation without sufficient support. This is why the larger reason many critics dismiss the resurrection is not their commitment to a particular theory but rather a commitment to naturalism. The debate is not largely about the historical facts but about how to interpret them. And worldview is at the heart of how people interpret the facts. If there is no God, then there *must* be a naturalistic explanation for the origin of the belief in the deity and resurrection of Jesus. But if we are open to the supernatural, then the resurrection becomes a much more reasonable explanation.

Before we move on from the case for the resurrection, there's one more piece of evidence to consider: the fate of the apostles.

CHAPTER 25

WERE THE APOSTLES MARTYRED FOR BELIEF IN THE RESURRECTION?

Even though they were crucified, stoned, stabbed, dragged, skinned, and burned, every last apostle of Jesus proclaimed his resurrection until their dying breath, refusing to recant under pressure from the authorities. Therefore, their testimony is trustworthy and the resurrection is true.

If you have followed popular arguments for the resurrection (or ever heard a sermon on the apostles), you've likely heard this argument. Growing up I (Sean) heard it regularly and found it quite convincing. After all, why would the apostles of Jesus have died for their faith if it weren't true?

Yet these questions were always in the back of my mind: How do we know they died as martyrs? And what would their deaths demonstrate about the truth of Christianity? To answer these questions, I spent over three years researching the traditions of the apostles for my PhD dissertation. Much of what follows comes from my academic book *The Fate of the Apostles.*

Keep an important point in mind: The willingness of the apostles to suffer and die for their faith doesn't prove the resurrection happened or that Christianity is true. It is part of a cumulative case for the resurrection that helps establish the sincerity of the apostles. It shows they weren't liars and that they truly believed Jesus had appeared to them after his death.

EVIDENCE FOR THE HISTORICITY OF THE APOSTLES' SUFFERING AND MARTYRDOM

If early Christians were persecuted for their faith, that would provide a helpful setting for evaluating the likelihood of the martyrdoms of individual apostles. Even though persecution was sporadic and local, there is evidence that the public proclamation of the faith could be costly. Jesus was crucified. Stephen was stoned to death after his witness before the Sanhedrin (Acts 6–8). And Herod Agrippa killed James the brother of John (Acts 12:2), which led to the departure of the rest of the Twelve from Jerusalem. The first statewide persecution of Christians was under Nero (AD 64), as reported by Tacitus and Suetonius.[1] The apostles publicly proclaimed the resurrection of a crucified criminal, with full awareness of what their actions might cost them.

The apostles would not have been surprised that they faced persecution. Jesus taught that his followers would suffer and be killed—as Israel had killed the prophets—for their proclamation of the name of Jesus (Matt. 5:10–11, 43–44; Mark 12:1–11; Luke 6:22–23). The expectation of suffering and persecution is a central theme throughout the New Testament, Old Testament, and pre-Christian Jewish literature such as 2 Maccabees. During the first century AD, there was an anticipation that prophets would suffer and die at the hands of their own people as well as secular authorities.

There is good reason to believe that the first Christians, including the apostles, suffered for their faith. But is there evidence that the apostles actually died as martyrs?

GENERAL CLAIMS FOR THE MARTYRDOM OF THE APOSTLES

Two church fathers provide early evidence for the tradition that some of Jesus's closest followers were martyred. First is Polycarp, bishop of Smyrna, who lived AD 69–155 and is said to have been a disciple of the apostle John. Second is Aphrahat, a Syriac Christian who lived in the late third to early fourth century.

Polycarp, *Letter to the Philippians*

> I exhort you all therefore to be obedient unto the word of righteousness and to practice all endurance, which also ye saw with your own eyes in the blessed Ignatius and Zosimus and Rufus, yea and in others also who came from among yourselves, as well as in Paul himself and the rest of the Apostles; being persuaded that all these *ran not in vain* but in faith and righteousness, and that they are in their due place in the presence of the Lord, with whom also they suffered. For they *loved not the present world*, but Him that died for our sakes and was raised by God for us.[2]

Aphrahat, *Demonstration 21: Of Persecution*

> Great and excellent is the martyrdom of Jesus. He surpassed in affliction and in confession all who were before or after. And after Him was the faithful martyr Stephen

whom the Jews stoned. Simon (Peter) also and Paul were perfect martyrs. And James and John walked in the footsteps of their Master Christ. Also (others) of the apostles thereafter in various places confessed and proved true martyrs.[3]

Admittedly, these citations are helpful but limited. For example, Polycarp mentions Paul and the rest of the apostles, but by "apostles," he clearly doesn't mean the Twelve because he considers Paul an apostle. Aphrahat mentions Stephen, Peter, Paul, James, and John as martyrs, but he wrote much later and at a significant geographical distance from the recorded events. Even so, these are two historical sources for the martyrdom of the apostles.

EVIDENCE FOR THE MARTYRDOM OF INDIVIDUAL APOSTLES

Now let's examine the evidence for each martyred apostle.

Peter

The traditional view is that Peter was crucified in Rome during the reign of Nero between AD 64 and 67. The earliest evidence for the martyrdom of Peter comes from John 21:18–19, which was likely written within three decades of Peter's death. Most commentators agree that this passage predicts the martyrdom of Peter. Another first-century reference to the martyrdom of Peter comes from Clement of Rome (1 Clement 5:1–4). Even Bart Ehrman concludes, "It is clear that Peter is being told that he will be executed (he won't die of natural causes) and that this will be the death of a martyr."[4] Some second-century sources for the martyrdom of Peter include Ignatius (*Letter to the Smyrnaeans* 3:1–2), Apocalypse of Peter, Ascension of Isaiah, Acts of Peter, Apocryphon of James, Dionysius of Corinth (Eusebius, *Ecclesiastical History* 2.25.4), Muratorian Canon, and Tertullian (*Scorpiace* 15, *Prescription against Heresies* 36). The early, consistent, and unanimous testimony is that Peter died a martyr.

Paul

The traditional view is that Paul was beheaded in Rome during the reign of Nero between AD 64 and 67. Scripture does not directly state his martyrdom, but hints in both Acts and 2 Timothy 4:6–8 show Paul knew his death was pending. This and other evidence throughout Acts and the Pauline letters (especially 2 Corinthians 11) show that Paul endured many sufferings and dangers on account of the gospel. The first extrabiblical evidence is found in 1 Clement 5:5–7 (ca. AD 95–96), in which Paul is described as suffering greatly for his faith and then being "set free from this world and transported up to the holy place, having become the greatest example of endurance." While details regarding the manner of his fate are lacking, the immediate context strongly implies that Clement was referring to the martyrdom of Paul. Other early sources for the martyrdom of Paul can be found in Ignatius (*Letter to the Ephesians* 12:2), Polycarp (*Letter to the Philippians* 9:1–2), Dionysius of Corinth (Eusebius, *Ecclesiastical History* 2.25.4), Irenaeus (*Against Heresies* 3.1.1), Acts of Paul, and Tertullian (*Scorpiace* 15:5–6). The early, consistent, and unanimous testimony is that Paul died a martyr.

James, Son of Zebedee

Only a few apocryphal accounts survive surrounding James, the son of Zebedee. The Acts of Saint James in India reports a tradition that he went to India along with Peter. The Apostolic History of Abdias (sixth and seventh centuries) tells a story of James and his interaction with two pagan magicians who eventually confess Christ. The most likely reason apocryphal accounts about James are rare and late is because his martyrdom in Judea (AD 44) was so firmly entrenched in the early church and limited the trajectory of such stories. His martyrdom is first recorded in Acts 12:1–2: "About that time Herod the king laid violent hands on some who belonged to the church. He killed James the brother of John with the sword" (ESV). The brevity of the account may be unexpected, but it does serve to strengthen its reliability. No legendary, flowery details creep into the narrative. Rather, quite the opposite is true. The account reads like an official execution notice. Although we have only one early source for the death of James, there is no good reason to doubt Luke's account of his death at the hands of Herod.

James, Brother of Jesus

The earliest evidence for the death of James comes from Josephus in his *Antiquities* 20.197–203 (ca. AD 93/94). Unlike the *Testimonium Flavianum* (*Antiquities of the Jews* 18.3.3), this passage is largely undisputed by scholars. It places the dating of James's execution to AD 62, since Josephus puts his death between the terms of two Roman procurators, Festus and Albinus. According to this account, the high priest Ananus had James stoned to death. Although some of the details vary, the death of James is also reported by Hegesippus (Eusebius,

Ecclesiastical History 2.23.8–18), Clement of Alexandria (*Hypotyposes* Book 7), *The First Apocalypse of James* (gnostic text), and the Pseudo-Clementines (*Recognitions* 1:66–1.71). The case for the martyrdom of James is strengthened by the fact that there are Christian sources (Hegesippus, Clement of Alexandria), Jewish sources (Josephus), and Gnostic sources (*First Apocalypse of James*) that affirm its occurrence within a century and a half of the event, which suggests an early, widespread, and consistent tradition regarding the fate of James.

COMMON OBJECTION TO THE APOLOGETIC VALUE OF THE APOSTLES' MARTYRDOMS

One of the most common responses to the deaths of the apostles is the claim that others dying for their beliefs neutralizes any significance of the apostles of Jesus dying for theirs. For instance, on September 11, 2001, nineteen radical Muslims hijacked four planes and, killing themselves in the process, attacked and killed thousands of people. Do their deaths provide equal credibility to their beliefs about Islam?

This objection misses a key difference between the deaths of the apostles and modern martyrs. Modern martyrs die for what they sincerely believe is true, but their knowledge comes secondhand from others. For instance, Muslim terrorists who attacked the Twin Towers on 9/11 were not eyewitnesses of any miracles by Muhammad. In fact, they were not eyewitnesses of *any* events of the life of Muhammad. Rather, they lived over thirteen centuries later. No doubt the Muslim radicals acted out of sincere belief, but their convictions were received secondhand at best. They did not know Muhammad personally, see him fulfill any prophecy, or witness him doing any miracles such as walking on water, healing the blind, or rising from the dead. There is a massive difference between willingly dying for the sake of the religious ideas accepted from the testimony of others (as in the case of the 9/11 terrorists) and willingly dying for the proclamation of a faith based on one's own eyewitness account (apostles). The deaths of the nineteen terrorists provide no more credibility for their beliefs than our sacrifices would provide for our beliefs. Our martyrdoms would show we really believed it, but unlike the apostles, we were not eyewitnesses to the resurrection of Jesus.

CONCLUSION

The willingness of the apostles to suffer and die for their faith does not *prove* the resurrection is true. But it does show the depth of the apostles' convictions that Jesus had risen and appeared to them. They were not liars. They did not invent the resurrection stories. The apostles proclaimed the risen Jesus to skeptical and antagonistic audiences with full knowledge they would likely suffer and possibly die for their beliefs. The evidence seems to indicate that the apostles willingly suffered for their beliefs, and we have good reason to believe some of them faced execution. There is no evidence they ever wavered. Their convictions were not based on secondhand testimony but personal experience with the risen Jesus, whom they truly believed was the risen Messiah—banking their lives on it. It is difficult to imagine what more a group of ancient witnesses could have done to show greater depth of sincerity and commitment to the truth of their beliefs.

SECTION 6

CONCLUSION

We believe that the resurrection is true, and the accounts of it have provided adequate evidence to certify it as a real event. The importance of the resurrection to the faith of the believer and the life of the church cannot be overstated. The apostle Paul suspends the entire weight of Christianity on the single thread of the historical resurrection of Jesus of Nazareth: "If Christ has not been raised, then our preaching is vain, your faith also is vain. . . . If Christ has not been raised, your faith is worthless; you are still in your sins. . . . If we have hoped in Christ only in this life, we are of all people most to be pitied" (1 Cor. 15:14, 17, 19 NASB).

Paul is clear: to lose the resurrection is to lose Christianity. As the resurrection goes, so goes Christianity. This is what makes this subject not just interesting but vitally important. Even the skeptics do not go so far as to deny the effects of the resurrection (the existence of the church and the new first-century meanings of baptism and communion as central sacramental rites). When they contest the recorded facts describing the burial and the empty tomb; or the narratives of the radically changed lives of the disciples after seeing the risen

Jesus; or the immediate and amazing conversions of James, Paul, more than three thousand on the day of Pentecost, and others named throughout the New Testament, their conclusions and claims spring from prior underlying assumptions. What the skeptics ultimately have an issue with is the supernatural component and the theological implications of the resurrection.

Both the skeptic and the Christian believe that dead people do not come back to life via natural means. This is why the skeptic must spend time coming up with alternate theories to explain the effects and the facts of the resurrection. On the other hand, the Christian can point to a supernatural event as the only viable explanation for the fact and effects of the resurrection: God raised Jesus from the dead.

While a single alternate theory might be capable of explaining just one piece of evidence, none of the alternate theories can account for all the evidence. Given all we know about the resurrection as a historical event, we must conclude with all those across the centuries who placed their confidence in the resurrected Christ and found their lives transformed: Christ is risen! He is risen indeed!

WHY THE RESURRECTION OF JESUS MATTERS

In this final section, we shift gears slightly. We will lay out the final pieces—final as far as the scope of this book is concerned—of historical evidence for Jesus. And we will conclude by examining why the resurrection of Jesus matters: If Jesus has really risen from the dead, what does it mean for my life? What does the resurrection say about the person of Jesus, as well as his teachings and claims? That is the subject of this section. Jesus's resurrection is more than just another religious miracle claim—it is the cornerstone of the Christian faith.

CHAPTER 26

WAS JESUS'S RESURRECTION PHYSICAL OR SPIRITUAL?

I (Sean) regularly take high school students on apologetics mission trips to engage skeptics, atheists, and people of other faiths. On one trip, our skeptical guest argued that the New Testament teaches that Jesus rose spiritually but not physically. Have you encountered people who appear to know a few things about Christianity but feel more comfortable with Jesus's resurrection as metaphorical rather than as a true historical event? Because of the evidence we've shared, you know that the Bible teaches Jesus rose physically. But does it matter? To put it simply, everything rests on Jesus rising *physically*.

Of course, we must now turn to the question, What is a resurrection? To answer that, let's first examine four common misconceptions.

RESURRECTION IS *NOT* REVIVAL

The Bible contains many instances of individuals being brought back to life. For example, Elisha raised the son of the Shunammite woman (2 Kings 4:35), Peter raised Tabitha (Acts 9:36–42), and Jesus raised his friend Lazarus (John

11:43–44). How are these revivals different from Jesus's resurrection?

What sets apart Jesus's coming back to life from all these other miraculous events of dead people being revived is that *they would eventually die again*—to be raised a final time with all those who belong to Christ at his second coming. The quality of their rising from the dead was something very different from the resurrection Jesus experienced. In addition to all this, Jesus's resurrected body had *new characteristics* that his preresurrection body did not possess. He was able to appear and disappear at will (Luke 24:31, 36–37, 51; John 20:19, 26), and he ascended to heaven in his physical body (Acts 1:6–11). None of these other people who were raised had yet received their resurrected bodies; they were raised in their mortal, flesh-and-blood bodies. This is why they were revived, not resurrected, while Jesus was resurrected in the fullest sense. And finally, these revivals were all the result of a power outside of the people raised to life. But Jesus was raised by his *own* power (John 2:19).

RESURRECTION IS *NOT* IMMORTALITY OF THE SOUL

Greek philosophers believed that the material world was corrupt and evil, so they viewed the body as a prison for the soul. Accordingly, the goal of salvation was to escape the physical realm and to be freed from bodily imprisonment. But ancient Hebrews and early Christians believed the material world was good, having been created by God. Resurrection is *not* a continuation of the soul without a body. The soul without a body is incomplete—a human being is the union of body *and* soul.

RESURRECTION IS *NOT* REINCARNATION

Eastern religions teach reincarnation: that people are reborn as someone—or some*thing*—else after their body dies. This act is considered a curse, not a blessing, as people must continually seek to improve themselves one life after the next. Depending on the specific tradition, the goal is to escape the cycle of reincarnation and experience nirvana or personal annihilation. This is *not* what the Bible means by resurrection. In contrast, the biblical view is that human beings live once and then are judged by God (Heb. 9:27).

RESURRECTION IS *NOT* TRANSLATION

The Bible records at least two instances where people were taken directly to God without dying. Enoch lived 365 years and then was taken away directly by God (Gen. 5:21–24). The prophet Elijah was taken to heaven by a whirlwind (2 Kings 2:1). These are not examples of resurrection because there is no evidence either man died; both were simply taken by God to heaven.

WHAT *IS* A RESURRECTION?

Now that we've addressed what resurrection is *not*, let's discuss what resurrection *is*. First off, what did "resurrection" mean to a first-century Jew? In short, it was a reversal of death. This does not mean that ancient people expected the reality of resurrection for themselves. But the concept of resurrection in antiquity consistently referred to a *physical* renewal of life, not some kind of immaterial continuation. So a modern critic who claims that Jesus's resurrection was merely metaphorical, or a spiritual rebirth, imposes a modern belief on ancient culture. Resurrection involved the physical body—period.

OBJECTION: PAUL SAID THE RESURRECTION IS JUST SPIRITUAL

In 1 Corinthians 15:44, Paul says that the body that is "sown" (dead and buried) is natural, while the body that is raised is spiritual. Then, in verse 50, he says that "flesh and blood cannot inherit the kingdom of God." Therefore, isn't Paul arguing that the resurrection is not physical but is immaterial? Is he contradicting the gospel writers who claimed Jesus was resurrected with "flesh and bones" (Luke 24:39)? Not at all. "Natural" and "spiritual" are not opposites. In verses 42–44, Paul is contrasting our weak, perishable bodies with the strong, imperishable bodies into which we will be resurrected. By "spiritual," Paul does not mean "immaterial," but "Spirit-filled." Our current bodies "run" on food and water, but our resurrection bodies will be powered by the Spirit.

Paul makes a similar comparison earlier in his letter. In 1 Corinthians 2:14–15, he discusses how the natural person does not understand the things of the Spirit of God, while the spiritual person does and so is able to judge God's teachings clearly. Here, the "natural" person is the one without the guidance of the Spirit, while the "spiritual" person is the one guided by the Spirit. With this distinction in mind, we see that Paul is not contrasting the physical with the immaterial in chapter 15. Rather he contrasts weak, earthly bodies with strong, Spirit-filled resurrection bodies. In both cases, the bodies are physical. But spiritual bodies will be filled with a power and glory, unlike our current weak, corruptible bodies, which are subject to decay. That is Paul's point.

CONCLUSION

In this chapter, we've learned what is meant by a resurrection, as well as what resurrection is *not*. Resurrection is not a reviv-ification back to one's former state of life. And it is not the immortality of the soul, reincarnation, or the translation of a person to heaven. Resurrection refers to the physical return of a person to life in a glorified, powerful, Spirit-filled body, never to die again.

Now that we understand what Jesus's resurrection *means*, let's explore why it *matters*.

CHAPTER 27

DID JESUS CLAIM HE WOULD RISE FROM THE DEAD?

NEAR THE BEGINNING OF THIS BOOK, WE LOOKED AT THE question of whether Jesus ever claimed to be God. This chapter considers a similar question: Did Jesus ever claim he would rise from the dead? Perhaps his followers placed words in Jesus's mouth and made claims about Jesus that he never made of himself.

Why does it matter if Jesus claimed he would rise from the dead? Isn't it good enough that he did? Resurrection claims are significant for several reasons. The fulfillment of these claims gives evidence that Jesus is not a false prophet. The Old Testament forewarned against unfulfilled claims from self-styled prophets: "When a prophet speaks in the name of the LORD, if the thing does not happen or come to pass, that is the thing which the LORD has not spoken; the prophet has spoken it presumptuously; you shall not be afraid of him" (Deut. 18:22).

So Jesus's predictions followed by evidence that the resurrection actually occurred strengthens our confidence that he is who he claimed to be—God incarnate:

> Then some of the scribes and Pharisees said to him,
> "Teacher, we want to see a sign from you."

He answered them, "An evil and adulterous generation demands a sign, but no sign will be given to it except
the sign of the prophet Jonah. For as Jonah was in the
belly of the huge fish three days and three nights, so the
Son of Man will be in the heart of the earth three days
and three nights. The men of Nineveh will stand up at the
judgment with this generation and condemn it, because
they repented at Jonah's preaching; and look—something
greater than Jonah is here. The queen of the south will rise
up at the judgment with this generation and condemn it,
because she came from the ends of the earth to hear the
wisdom of Solomon; and look—something greater than
Solomon is here. (Matt. 12:38–42)

Jesus Christ our Lord, who was born of the seed of David
according to the flesh, and declared to be the Son of God
with power according to the Spirit of holiness, by the resurrection from the dead. (Rom. 1:3–4)

To make a full case for the resurrection, it is important to
demonstrate that Jesus personally claimed he would rise on
the third day and that his followers did not invent the claims.
Let's take a look at the evidence that Jesus predicted his own
resurrection.

JESUS PREDICTED HIS OWN RESURRECTION

Jesus not only predicted his resurrection but also directed the
disciples as to what they should expect and do after it happened. When the Jewish authorities demanded a sign of his

authority, he responded in terms that the disciples afterward understood as a fulfillment of an Old Testament type.

> From that time Jesus began to show to His disciples that He must go to Jerusalem, and suffer many things from the elders and chief priests and scribes, and be killed, and be raised the third day. (Matt. 16:21)

> As they came down from the mountain, Jesus commanded them, saying, "Tell the vision to no one until the Son of Man is risen from the dead." (Matt. 17:9)

> While they were staying in Galilee, Jesus said to them, "The Son of Man is about to be betrayed into the hands of men, and they will kill Him, and the third day He will be raised up." And they were exceedingly sorrowful. (Matt. 17:22–23)

> "Behold, we are going up to Jerusalem, and the Son of Man will be betrayed to the chief priests and to the scribes; and they will condemn Him to death, and deliver Him to the Gentiles to mock and to scourge and to crucify. And the third day He will rise again." (Matt. 20:18–19)

> "After I have been raised, I will go before you to Galilee." (Matt. 26:32)

> As they came down from the mountain, He commanded them that they should tell no one the things they had seen,

till the Son of Man had risen from the dead. So they kept this word to themselves, questioning what the rising from the dead meant. (Mark 9:9–10)

"The Son of Man must suffer many things, and be rejected by the elders and chief priests and scribes, and be killed, and be raised the third day."

Then He said to them all, "If anyone desires to come after Me, let him deny himself, and take up his cross daily, and follow Me. For whoever desires to save his life will lose it, but whoever loses his life for My sake will save it. For what profit is it to a man if he gains the whole world, and is himself destroyed or lost? For whoever is ashamed of Me and My words, of him the Son of Man will be ashamed when He comes in His own glory, and in His Father's, and of the holy angels. But I tell you truly, there are some standing here who shall not taste death till they see the kingdom of God." (Luke 9:22–27)

The Jews replied to Him, "What sign of authority will You show us for doing these things?"

Jesus answered, "Destroy this sanctuary, and I will raise it up in three days."

Therefore the Jews said, "This sanctuary took 46 years to build, and will You raise it up in three days?"

But He was speaking about the sanctuary of His body. So when He was raised from the dead, His disciples remembered that He had said this. And they believed the Scripture and the statement Jesus had made. (John 2:18–22)

These passages clearly indicate that Jesus predicted his resurrection. Skeptics might still wonder whether we can trust them as reliable historical claims since they were written by his followers years later. But a careful comparison of these passages helps answer this dilemma in the affirmative.

The gospels of Matthew and Mark report that a rumor was circulating, which was used at the trial of Jesus, that Jesus would destroy the temple and rebuild it in three days, but not with human hands (Mark 14:57–59; Matt. 26:60–61). Matthew and Mark allude to this saying but leave the reader hanging as to what Jesus actually said. Nothing in either of these gospels provides a pretext for this serious allegation. John 2:19 supplies the original statement from Jesus, though John does not report its later use as an accusation against Jesus. Thus, neither of these appears to be copied from the other, and thus this "undesigned coincidence" confirms the historicity of the saying.

We see in many verses that Jesus claimed he would die and rise again. Because the claims were so audacious, many of his hearers did not entirely understand what he meant at the time. In Mark 8:31–33, Peter rebukes Jesus after hearing Jesus predict his death and resurrection. In turn, Jesus rebukes Peter for rejecting what Jesus told him. This is significant because the embarrassing nature of the exchange makes it unlikely that it was an invention of the early church. Also, this text refers to Jesus as "Son of Man," which is Jesus's favorite divine title for himself, one the early church did not use. This adds to the authenticity of the passage.

Communion, or the Lord's Supper, is an important Christian commemorative practice. When Jesus instituted this ceremony at the famous Last Supper, he directly referenced his death through the breaking of his body (the bread) and the spilling of his blood (the wine). But as noted, Jesus follows this event by mentioning his coming kingdom (Luke 22:29) and plans to meet the disciples in Galilee after his resurrection (Mark 14:28). So one of Christianity's most famous practices links to Jesus predicting not only his death but also his resurrection.

CONCLUSION

Not only was Jesus aware of his mission, but he made it known to others as well. Jesus implicitly and explicitly made known that he was aware of his impending death and resurrection. This was no mere unfortunate incident or course correction of God's grand design. This was the plan all along. Jesus came to die and rise again to save the world.

CHAPTER 28

DOES THE RESURRECTION RELATE TO JESUS'S DEITY?

WE PREVIOUSLY EXPLORED THE DEITY OF CHRIST AS WELL as the evidence for the historicity of Jesus's resurrection. Now we will see how the two are connected: Jesus's resurrection confirms that Jesus is indeed God in the flesh.

JESUS COULD HAVE ESCAPED CRUCIFIXION

Jesus was a brilliant thinker and performed many wondrous miracles in his lifetime. Surely he could have found a way to avoid his crucifixion, miraculously or otherwise. Even Jesus's enemies admitted this point in a backhanded way. While Jesus hung on the cross, some of the chief priests and scribes mocked Jesus by saying to one another, "He saved others; Himself He cannot save" (Mark 15:31). Their taunt implicitly acknowledged that Jesus was known to have miraculously saved others from death. Even if one supposes that it would have been too difficult for Jesus to get down from the cross—a claim the Gospels do not support—surely Jesus could have saved himself from being crucified in the first place. All he would have needed to do was perform some miracle for the benefit of the Jewish or Roman authorities.

Jesus did not use miraculous power to escape from the cross, because he came to die for our sins, as he indicates in Mark 10:45: "The Son of Man did not come to be served, but to serve, and to give His life a ransom for many" (see also Matt. 26:53–54; John 10:17–18).

Allowing himself to be captured, tried, and executed communicates the heart of his mission: *to redeem humanity and usher in the kingdom of God.* The Christian belief in the death of Jesus is not a later myth that seeped into the church or an accidental fact of history. Rather, it is the culmination of the Old Testament teaching that sacrifice is necessary for forgiveness. As an act of love and redemption, *Jesus chose to die.*

Jesus's resurrection confirms that Jesus indeed chose to accept crucifixion for God's purpose.

JESUS'S RESURRECTION VINDICATED HIS INNOCENCE AND HIS DIVINE MISSION

Jesus's death by crucifixion must have seemed to his disciples, in the dark hours that followed, to call into question everything they had believed about him. Crucifixion was not an honorable death. Far from it: crucifixion was designed to be the most shameful way to die. The victim was typically stripped naked and exposed near a public thoroughfare. He would suffer in agony for hours, finding it increasingly difficult to breathe. Also, the law of Moses said that "he who is hanged is accursed of God" (Deut. 21:23), or as the Greek Septuagint put it, "anyone hung on a tree is under God's curse" (Deut. 21:23 HCSB). No wonder the two disciples on the road to Emmaus spoke of their faith in Jesus in the past tense: "We *were hoping* that it was He who was going to redeem Israel" (Luke 24:21, emphasis added). Jesus's shameful death must have seemed to discredit all his claims. The Sanhedrin—the Jewish council led by the chief priest—had apparently been right in viewing Jesus as a blasphemer. The resurrection of Jesus changed all that.

In the first Christian sermon, the apostle Peter affirmed that Jesus was "a man attested to you by God with mighty works and wonders and signs that God did through him in your midst, as you yourselves know" (Acts 2:22 ESV). Despite the clear testimony of the miracles, the Jewish authorities had handed him over to the Romans to be crucified. But "God raised him up" (2:24 ESV). Jesus's resurrection vindicated him as God's "Holy One" (2:27 ESV) and revealed him to be "both Lord and Christ" (2:36 ESV).

The apostle Paul expressed this same idea in his epistle to the Romans. The gospel is the message of God "concerning his Son, who was descended from David according to the flesh and was declared to be the Son of God in power according to the Spirit of holiness by his resurrection from the dead, Jesus Christ our Lord" (Rom. 1:3–4 ESV). Jesus's resurrection was divine vindication that he was the Savior of Israel and of the entire world.

JESUS'S RESURRECTION MAKES HIS VIRGIN BIRTH CREDIBLE

When we discussed the virgin birth of Jesus Christ, we said it could not be proved historically since there was only one human witness, Mary herself. But we claimed that the virgin birth was not a later legend or myth but was part of the earliest Christian traditions about Jesus, probably originating from Jesus's family members. This evidence alone is perhaps not enough to convince a skeptic—even an open-minded one— that the virgin birth is historical fact. However, the virgin birth does not stand on its own. It fits within the context of the early church's testimony about the person who performed amazing miracles during his mortal lifetime and rose from the dead to immortality. In the context of Jesus's miraculous ministry and especially his miraculous resurrection, his virgin birth looks far more credible than it would otherwise.

We are not arguing that the virgin birth is as central to the Christian message as the resurrection or that if you believe in the resurrection, then you must automatically also believe in the virgin birth. Rather, the point is that the resurrection shows that the entire story of Jesus in the Gospels, which includes his birth to a virgin, is consistent with what the resurrection reveals about Jesus. The two make sense together.

In the virgin birth, the Son of God comes down from heaven, humbling himself to take our frail form, and eventually suffers the ultimate humiliation in the crucifixion. In the resurrection, the Son of God comes up from the grave— exchanging his frail form for a new immortal body—ascends to heaven, and is glorified and exalted.

CONCLUSION: THE HYPOTHESIS CONFIRMED

For the sake of simplicity, consider two rival hypotheses:

Hypothesis 1

Jesus was a good teacher, perhaps something of a prophet, who ran afoul of the political authorities and was executed. As the years passed after his death, legends developed about Jesus performing miracles and rising from the dead, even being born of a virgin. These legendary elements eventually led to the belief that Jesus was God incarnate. In short, the early church invented claims of deity for Jesus and the stories that supported those claims.

Hypothesis 2

Jesus was a teacher but an extraordinary one, performing miracles that astounded the people. He also made divine claims for himself in connection with these miracles, claims that the Jewish authorities considered blasphemous. They had him arrested and handed over to the Roman authorities, who crucified him as a potential threat to order. He then rose from the dead, appeared to his followers, and ascended to heaven. The community of believers he left behind, which included members of his family, preserved their recollections of the things Jesus had said and done. His family passed on to others their own stories, including that Jesus's mother Mary was a virgin when he was born. As the early church reflected on what they knew about Jesus, they understood that he was the divine Son of God who had come down from heaven. In short, the early church accepted Jesus's claims to deity in light of the evidence that supported those claims, especially his resurrection.

Which hypothesis about Jesus is best supported by the evidence? Let's review the evidence we have surveyed in this section and the previous one, beginning with the resurrection.

1. The resurrection of Jesus is a historical event for which we have strong evidence. It vindicates Jesus's claims to be the divine Messiah and establishes the credibility of the gospel accounts of Jesus as a supernatural figure.

2. Examining the Gospels even in a fairly critical fashion, biblical scholars now widely agree that Jesus performed exorcisms and healings that were understood by everyone in his society as miraculous or supernatural.

3. Jesus was an honorable, innocent man who was ahead of his time in his moral vision; the criticisms that his contemporaries made against him were either false accusations or faulted him for challenging their limited cultural attitudes in ways that we can see today were admirable.

4. Finally, the accounts in Matthew and Luke of Jesus's conception and virgin birth provide independent testimonies to that fact, probably stemming from Joseph and Mary themselves. They are not plausibly explained as imitating pagan stories of gods impregnating mortal women or as fictions composed to present Jesus as the fulfillment of Old Testament prophecy. The best explanation for these accounts is that they go back to the experience of Mary herself. In light of Jesus's miracles and resurrection, the virgin birth is certainly consistent with everything else we know about Jesus.

Considering these findings, the hypothesis that Jesus really was the divine Son of God come in the flesh does a far better job of explaining the evidence than the hypothesis that he was a good teacher whom the early church divinized after his tragic death. The resurrection is the final confirmation that Jesus is the unique Son of God.

CHAPTER 29

WHY DOES THE RESURRECTION MATTER?

IN THIS CHAPTER, WE ARE GOING TO GET PRACTICAL. WHILE apologetics is vital for defending the faith, we must also see how the resurrection shapes our relationship with God and how we confront death. The impact of the resurrection cannot be overstated. Let's start briefly with Paul's words about the importance of the resurrection.

IF CHRIST IS NOT RAISED, THEN NOTHING ELSE MATTERS

Paul weaves together a tight argument in 1 Corinthians 15:12–19. Without the resurrection, we would lose a foundation for faith, trust in the veracity of the apostles, redemption from sin, and hope for resurrection of our loved ones and ourselves. We would be supremely pitiable.

No other religion is based on the resurrection of its founder. Jesus's resurrection is the core of the Christian worldview. The Gospels do not end at the death of Jesus. If so, the disciples would have remained despondent and defeated. Even if they had continued his teachings, they would still have no

Messiah. The crucifixion would have ended everything. But the Gospels do not end there. After Jesus's death, the story continues with an empty tomb, Jesus's appearances, and the final commission to his followers.

Jesus's resurrection is the cornerstone of the Christian faith. If there is no resurrection, there is no Christianity, period. I (Josh) have had more than one hundred debates with non-Christians about the reliability of the Christian faith. In nearly every debate, I raise this challenge to my opponent: "If you want to win this debate and refute me, all you have to do is refute the resurrection of Christ. If you can do that, Christianity crumbles and I would become a laughingstock."

THE RESURRECTION AND CHRISTIAN DOCTRINE

Finally, Jesus's resurrection empowers or energizes Christian teachings that without the resurrection would be hollow:

- ✦ Sending of the Spirit (Acts 2:32–33)
- ✦ Conversion of sinners (Acts 3:26)
- ✦ Forgiveness of sins (Acts 5:30–31)
- ✦ Freedom from the penalty and power of sin (Acts 13:37–39)
- ✦ God's judgment of the world (Acts 17:31)

Jesus's resurrection is not just another biblical miracle. The resurrection has a great impact on the life of the believer. It is *the* central miracle of the Christian faith. It guarantees our salvation (Rom. 10:9), gives us strength and hope, and secures our future resurrection. The resurrection means that Jesus is alive, and he is still with us today. No matter what you're going through, you are never alone. And if you're a follower of Christ, the same power that raised Jesus from the dead dwells within you too (Rom. 8:11).

THE RESURRECTION COMFORTS US IN OUR DOUBT AND GRIEF

Jesus's resurrection is much more than a historical event. The power of the resurrection is ongoing and meant to offer daily support to those who follow Jesus. A prime example of this is my (Sean's) own experience with doubt. As a college student, I went through a season of painful doubt when I encountered some sophisticated arguments against Christianity. Even though my parents had taught me how to defend my faith, I didn't have answers to a number of objections and distinctly remember thinking, "If I leave my faith, this could be very painful and costly." One of the things that grounded me during this season was the evidence for the resurrection. I couldn't find a better explanation for the historical facts we have discussed in this book. I realized that no matter what doubts we may struggle with, if Jesus has risen from the dead, then we can rest in the truth that Jesus is God. When I have doubts today, I often ask myself, "Did Jesus rise from the dead?" If the answer is yes, and I believe it is, then it helps put my doubts, questions, and struggles into perspective.

The resurrection can also provide hope during times of grief. Professor Gary Habermas is one of the leading resurrection experts in the world. His book *The Risen Jesus and Future Hope* includes an entire chapter about Gary's personal experience with how Jesus's resurrection helped him through the pain of losing his wife of twenty-three years to stomach cancer. While she suffered, he would frequently remind himself that even though he didn't know why this was happening to her, "this is still the same world in which God raised Jesus from the dead. Eternal life for believers is the direct result of this great event. Therefore, I can still trust God that there is a sufficient answer here, even if I do not know what it is. At the very worst, I will see Debbie again in heaven."[1]

In that last line, Habermas echoes 1 Thessalonians 4:13–18, in which Paul writes about those who have died in Christ. He says we do not grieve like those who have no hope, but since we believe that Jesus died and rose again, we can be confident that we will once more see our loved ones who were followers of Christ. While we will certainly grieve the loss of loved ones and mourn that they are no longer with us in this present life, we can still have confident hope that we will be reunited with them.

CONCLUSION

Christianity without the resurrection is false. Christians are not given the power of the Holy Spirit if there is no resurrection. People are still in their sins if there is no resurrection. The resurrection of Jesus is the defining historical event that establishes the truth of Christianity. It is the key to experiencing the Christian life. Because the resurrection is true, and we believe it, we can experience the power and freedom of Christ.

CHAPTER 30

FINAL WORDS OF ENCOURAGEMENT

Thanks for joining us on this journey. If you've stayed with us for this long, we're guessing that you have even more questions. Questions are not only okay but a good part of the Christian life. Jesus calls us to love God with our minds and to seek answers (Mark 12:30)! One thing we have both learned is that, if we are willing to do our homework, there are good answers for the toughest challenges to the Christian faith.

If you have nagging doubts, we want you to know you are not alone. Jude said to have mercy on those who doubt (v. 22). Why would he say this? For one, doubt can be a normal part of the Christian life. Especially today, in our age of limitless information in the palms of our hands, doubts are almost inevitable. The question is not whether we have doubts but how we address them. If you have further questions about Jesus, our book *Evidence That Demands a Verdict* may be a helpful next step.

Second, doubt can be painful. As a college student, I (Sean) went through a painful period of doubt. Nagging questions simply wouldn't go away. Rather than basing my faith on the opinions of others, I wanted a faith based on fact. At times these questions led me to feel the despair that existentialist writers such as Albert Camus and Jean-Paul Sartre said follows from the nonexistence of God. I remember staying up late at night reading the psalms of David as he wondered why God seemed so absent in his time of need.

As I wrestled with the big questions of life, I realized there was one person I needed to be honest with—my father. How would this great apologist react to his own son questioning the faith he so deeply cherished? As we sat at a small café in the mountains of Breckenridge, Colorado, I told my dad about my doubts. His response took me by surprise. "I think it's great that you want to find truth," he said. "It's wise not to accept things just because you were told them. You need to find out if Christianity is true. You know that your mom and I love you regardless of what you conclude. Seek after truth and take to heart the things your mom and I have taught you. And let me know if I can help along the way."

And that's exactly what I have tried to do. I started reading books by Christian apologists and by skeptics. I had to read as much of both sides as possible. After much thought, deliberation, and soul-searching, I concluded that my faith was well grounded. The evidence in this book is part of what persuaded me.

Yet it wasn't solely the historical evidence that I found persuasive. It was also Jesus's profound insight into the human condition that humbled me. Jesus said all kinds of wickedness come from within the human heart (Mark 7:21–23). Thus, the core problem with the world, according to Jesus, is not economic inequality (à la Marxism) or our forgetfulness that we are divine (New Age) but the wickedness of the human heart. As Frank Sinatra observed, we want to do it our way.

Although I was a pretty good kid growing up (i.e., I didn't

do any of the "big" sins), I began to realize the depths of my own pride and rebellion against God. I, too, needed a savior. Even though I had been in a Christian family my entire life, the message of Christ reached my heart like never before. I still have questions. And I still make mistakes. But following Jesus has been the best decision of my life.

We encourage you to share your doubts with others and to seek answers, just like we did. Jesus promised us, "Seek, and you will find" (Matt. 7:7). But as you search for truth, please don't ever be discouraged. Remember, God has mercy for those who doubt (Jude v. 22).

Finally, we hope you will share what you have found with others. If you are a Christian, consider sharing the evidence for Jesus with a friend, a coworker, your family, or non-Christians in your life.

CONCLUSION

WE'VE EXAMINED THE CASE FOR THE DEITY OF CHRIST, AND we've examined the evidence for the resurrection. And in this section, we've seen that the two are intertwined—Jesus's death and resurrection are the ultimate confirmation that he is indeed the Son of God. His rising from the dead is not just another miracle, like feeding the multitudes or walking on water, however. The resurrection is the cornerstone of the Christian faith. It launched the worldwide spread of the gospel and is the core of New Testament doctrine. It offers believers comfort, hope, and strength in this life and secures our future resurrection.

NOTES

Chapter 1: Can We Use the Bible for Historical Evidence of Jesus?

1. Bart D. Ehrman, *Did Jesus Exist? The Historical Argument for Jesus of Nazareth* (New York: HarperOne, 2012), 93.
2. Paul Rhodes Eddy and Gregory A. Boyd, *The Jesus Legend: A Case for the Historical Reliability of the Synoptic Jesus Tradition* (Grand Rapids: Baker Academic, 2007), 209.

Chapter 2: Is There Evidence for Jesus Outside the Bible?

1. Tacitus, *Annals* 15.44, http://www.perseus.tufts.edu/hopper /text?doc=Perseus%3Atext%3A1999.02.0078%3Abook%3D15 %3Achapter%3D44.
2. Paul Rhodes Eddy and Gregory A. Boyd, *The Jesus Legend: A Case for the Historical Reliability of the Synoptic Jesus Tradition* (Grand Rapids: Baker Academic, 2007), 181–82.
3. See *Josephus' Complete Works*, trans. William Whiston (Grand Rapids: Kregel, 1960), 645.
4. There is some debate over this exact number.
5. Eddy and Boyd, *The Jesus Legend*, 185–90.
6. John P. Meier, *A Marginal Jew: Rethinking the Historical Jesus*, vol. 1 (New York: Doubleday, 1991), 61.

Chapter 3: Are There Christian Sources for Jesus Outside the Bible?

1. Clement of Rome, 1 Clement 42:1–4, http://www.earlychristian writings.com/text/1clement-lightfoot.html.
2. Ignatius, *Letter to the Trallians* 9:1–2, http://www.earlychristian writings.com/text/ignatius-trallians-lightfoot.html.
3. Ignatius, *Letter to the Smyrnaeans* 1:1, 3:1–3, http://www.early christianwritings.com/text/ignatius-smyrnaeans-lightfoot.html.

4. Ignatius, *Letter to the Magnesians* 11:1, http://www.earlychristian writings.com/text/ignatius-magnesians-lightfoot.html.

5. Bart D. Ehrman, *Did Jesus Exist? The Historical Argument for Jesus of Nazareth* (New York: HarperOne, 2012), 103–104.

6. Irenaeus, *Against Heresies*, Book 3, 3.4, http://earlychristianwritings .com/text/irenaeus-book3.html.

7. Polycarp, *Epistle of Polycarp*, http://earlychristianwritings.com/text /polycarp-lightfoot.html.

8. Eusebius, *Church History* 3.39.2, https://www.newadvent.org /fathers/250103.htm.

9. Eusebius, *Church History* 3.39.4, 7.

10. Eusebius, *Church History* 3.39.15–16.

Chapter 4: Is the New Testament Reliable?

1. J. Warner Wallace, "Why I Know the Story of Jesus Wasn't Changed Over Time," Cold Case Christianity, March 24, 2017, https://cold casechristianity.com/writings/why-i-know-the-story-of-jesus-wasnt -changed-over-time/.

Section 1 Conclusion

1. Bart D. Ehrman, *Did Jesus Exist? The Historical Argument for Jesus of Nazareth* (New York: HarperOne, 2012), 171–173.

Chapter 8: Was Jesus Merely a Prophet or a Good Person?

1. C. S. Lewis, *Mere Christianity* (New York: Macmillan/Collier, 1952), 55–56.

2. Clark H. Pinnock, *Set Forth Your Case* (Nutley, NJ: Craig Press, 1967), 62.

Chapter 9: What Is Unique about Jesus's Life and Teachings?

1. See Ronald H. Nash, *The Gospel and the Greeks: Did the New Testament Borrow from Pagan Thought?*, 2nd ed. (Phillipsburg, NJ: P&R, 2003).

Chapter 10: What Is Unique about Jesus's Miracles?

1. Lewis, *Miracles: A Preliminary Study* (New York: Macmillan, 1947, 2nd ed. 1978), 108.

2. Craig S. Keener, *Miracles: The Credibility of the New Testament Accounts* (Grand Rapids: Baker Academic, 2011), 19, 23.

3. See Rudolf Bultmann, *Jesus and the Word*, trans. Louise Pettibone Smith and Erminie Huntress (New York: Charles Scribner's Sons, 1958, originally published 1934), 173; Joachim Jeremias, *New Testament Theology: The Proclamation of Jesus* (New York: Scribner, 1971), 92.

4. Josephus, *Antiquities of the Jews*, 18.3.3 §63.

5. See Craig S. Keener, *Miracles: The Credibility of the New Testament Accounts*, vol. 1 (Grand Rapids: Baker Academic, 2011), 25.

Chapter 13: What Are the Features of Mystery Religions?

1. The content of this chapter is deeply indebted to Ronald H. Nash, *The Gospel and the Greeks: Did the New Testament Borrow from Pagan Thought?* (Philipsburg, NJ: P&R, 2003).

Section 4 Conclusion

1. Bart Ehrman, "The Historical Jesus Did Exist," Abrahamic Faith, April 9, 2016, YouTube video, 2:34, https://youtu.be/43mDuI N5-ww.

Chapter 21: Are Miracles Possible?

1. As cited in Stephen C. Meyer, *Return of the God Hypothesis: Three Scientific Discoveries That Reveal the Mind Behind the Universe* (New York: HarperOne, 2021), 357–58.

2. J. P. Moreland, *A Simple Guide to Experience Miracles: Instruction and Inspiration for Living Supernaturally in Christ* (Grand Rapids: Zondervan, 2021), 126–30.

3. Moreland, *A Simple Guide to Experience Miracles*, 131–33.

4. Moreland, *A Simple Guide to Experience Miracles*, 122–23.

Chapter 22: What Are the Facts of the Resurrection?

1. W. D. Edwards, W. J. Gabel, and F. E. Hosmer, "On the Physical Death of Jesus Christ," *Journal of the American Medical Association* 255, vol. 11 (March 21, 1986): 1463, https://pubmed.ncbi.nlm.nih.gov/3512867/.

2. Gerd Lüdemann, *The Resurrection of Christ: A Historical Inquiry* (Amherst, NY: Prometheus, 2004), 50.

3. John Dominic Crossan, *Jesus: A Revolutionary Biography* (New York: HarperSanFrancisco, 1994), 145.

4. Bart D. Ehrman, "Why Was Jesus Killed?," *The Bart Ehrman Blog: The History & Literature of Early Christianity* (blog), October 16, 2012, http://ehrmanblog.org/why-was-jesus-killed/.

5. John Dominic Crossan, *The Historical Jesus: The Life of a Mediterranean Jewish Peasant* (New York: HarperSanFrancisco, 1992), 372.

Chapter 24: Three More Alternative Explanations for the Resurrection

1. "Debunking the Hallucination Hypothesis: Leading Doctors Speak on Jesus," Dr. Sean McDowell, YouTube video, 58:00, https://www.youtube.com/watch?v=iT12FnjJLKI.

2. "Debunking the Hallucination Hypothesis," quote at 26:00.

3. Frank Larøi et al., "An Epidemiological Study on the Prevalence of Hallucinations in a General-Population Sample: Effects of Age and Sensory Modality," *Psychiatry Research*, vol. 272 (February 2019): 707–14, https://doi.org/10.1016/j.psychres.2019.01.003.

4. "Debunking the Hallucination Hypothesis," quote at 27:38. In the YouTube interview, we focused on the probability of middle-aged men (31–60) experiencing hallucinations. There is a .8% prevalence rate for men in this age range. For this book, we consider prevalence rates for the likely age range of the apostles (19–31).

5. "Debunking the Hallucination Hypothesis," quote at 38:00.

6. "Debunking the Hallucination Hypothesis," quote at 41:27.

Chapter 25: Were the Apostles Martyred for Belief in the Resurrection?

1. Tacitus, *Annals* 15.44:2–5; Suetonius, *Nero* 16.2.

2. Polycarp, *Letter to the Philippians* 9:1–2, http://earlychristian writings.com/text/polycarp-lightfoot.html.

3. Aphrahat, *Demonstration XXI: Of Persecution* 23.

4. Bart D. Ehrman, *Peter, Paul, and Mary Magdalene: The Followers of Jesus in History and Legend* (Oxford: Oxford University Press, 2006), 84.

Chapter 29: Why Does the Resurrection Matter?

1. Gary Habermas, *The Risen Jesus and Future Hope* (Lanham, MD: Rowman & Littlefield, 2003), 192.